T0164610

WHEN LINCOLN CAME TO EGYPT

A SHAWNEE CLASSIC

WHEN LINCOLN CAME TO EGYPT

GEORGE W. SMITH

With a Foreword by Daniel W. Stowell

Southern Illinois University Press
Carbondale

Southern Illinois University Press
www.siupress.com

Copyright © 2016 by the Board of Trustees,
Southern Illinois University
Foreword copyright © 2016 by Daniel W. Stowell
All rights reserved. Trovillion Private Press edition 1940.
Southern Illinois University Press edition 2016
Printed in the United States of America

19 18 17 16   4 3 2 1

Cover illustration: image of Abraham Lincoln reproduced from a daguerreotype given by President Lincoln to General William Livingston Scott and subsequently passed to Scott's cousin Hattie Maxwell Burke, who gave it to her daughter, Lulu Burke Nave, who allowed the author to use it as a frontispiece in the 1940 Trovillion Private Press edition. Background map, "Indiana, Illinois, Missouri & Iowa with Parts of Adjoining States" (New York: G. Woolworth Colton; agent, Chicago, Rufus Blanchard, 1858), Library of Congress.

Library of Congress Cataloging-in-Publication Data
Names: Smith, George Washington, 1855–1945, author.
Title: When Lincoln came to Egypt / George W. Smith ; with a foreword by
    Daniel W. Stowell.
Description: Carbondale : Southern Illinois University Press, 2016. | Origi-
    nally published: Herrin, Illinois : Trovillion Private Press, 1940.
Identifiers: LCCN 2016027058| ISBN 9780809335527 (paperback) | ISBN
    9780809335534 (e-book)
Subjects: LCSH: Lincoln, Abraham, 1809–1865—Travel—Illinois. | Lincoln,
    Abraham, 1809–1865—Political career before 1861. | Politicians—
    Illinois—Biography. | Political candidates—Illinois—Biography. |
    Lincoln-Douglas Debates, Ill., 1858. | Douglas, Stephen A. (Stephen
    Arnold), 1813–1861. | Illinois—Politics and government—To 1865.
    | Jonesboro (Ill.) —Politics and government—19th century. | BISAC:
    HISTORY / United States / State & Local / Midwest (IA, IL, IN, KS,
    MI, MN, MO, ND, NE, OH, SD, WI). | HISTORY / United States /
    19th Century.
Classification: LCC E457.3 .S68 2016 | DDC 973.7092 [B] —dc23
LC record available at https://lccn.loc.gov/2016027058

Printed on recycled paper. ♻

DEDICATION

THIS LITTLE VOLUME IS DEDICATED TO THE THOUSANDS OF YOUNG MEN AND YOUNG WOMEN WHO WERE ENROLLED IN MY CLASSES IN THE SOUTHERN ILLINOIS STATE NORMAL COLLEGE IN THE FORTY-FIVE YEARS OF MY ACTIVE SERVICE AS A TEACHER IN THAT BELOVED INSTITUTION.

MANY OF THESE FORMER STUDENTS ARE NOW OCCUPYING POSITIONS OF HONOR, TRUST, AND RESPONSIBILITY IN ALL THE WALKS OF OUR COMMON LIFE. I STILL COUNT THEM MY FRIENDS AND CO-WORKERS IN THE TASK OF ADVANCING THE WELL-BEING AND IN PERPETUATING THE GLORY OF EGYPT.

CARRY ON.

THE AUTHOR.

CONTENTS

	Page
LIST OF ILLUSTRATIONS	ix
FOREWORD, *Daniel W. Stowell*	xi
INTRODUCTION, *Paul M. Angle*	xvii
AUTHOR'S PREFACE, *George W. Smith*	xix
THOSE WHO HAVE HELPED	xxiii
WHEN LINCOLN CAME TO EGYPT, *George W. Smith*	
WHENCE CAME THE EGYPTIANS	1
LINCOLN IN PUBLIC LIFE	9
THE KANSAS-NEBRASKA BILL	13
RISE OF THE REPUBLICAN PARTY	17
KANSAS—SLAVE OR FREE	21
DOUGLAS TRIUMPHANT	25
TWO GREAT LEADERS	29
THIS SECTION CALLED EGYPT	33
LINCOLN'S FRIENDS IN EGYPT	39
LINCOLN IN EGYPT	45
SOME TRADITIONS	107
THE BATTLE BEGINS	111
DOUGLAS EN ROUTE	113
LINCOLN EN ROUTE	119
AT THE DEBATE	127
THE DEBATE	131
LINCOLN REPLIES	135
DOUGLAS CLOSES	141
THE DEPARTURE	143
A SHORT SAD CAREER	149
A TRAGIC ENDING	153
INDEX—PERSONS AND PLACES	157

ILLUSTRATIONS

Facing Page

1 FRONTISPIECE—PRESIDENT LINCOLN ABOUT 1864

2 LINCOLN MEMORIAL, MARKING WHERE LINCOLN
FIRST SET FOOT ON ILLINOIS SOIL   9

3 BOWMAN HOTEL, ALBION, ILLINOIS, WHERE LIN-
COLN WAS ENTERTAINED SEPTEMBER, 1840 . .   17

4 THE JOEL LACKEY HOME, NEAR PULASKI, ILLINOIS,
WHERE LINCOLN STAYED OVERNIGHT . . .   25

5 SITE OF THE LINCOLN-DOUGLAS DEBATE . . .   33

6 THE PHILLIPS HOME, ANNA, ILLINOIS, WHERE LIN-
COLN WAS GUEST   65

7 JOHN A. LOGAN HOME, BENTON, ILLINOIS, WHERE
DOUGLAS WAS ENTERTAINED SEPTEMBER 16, 1858   97

8 HORACE WHITE, EDITOR CHICAGO TRIBUNE, WHO
ACCOMPANIED LINCOLN DURING DEBATES . .   113

9 HENRY EDDY, SHAWNEETOWN, ILLINOIS, EDITOR
OF THE EMIGRANT   129

10 LINCOLN MEMORIAL ON PUBLIC SQUARE, FAIR-
FIELD, ILLINOIS   153

FOREWORD

DANIEL W. STOWELL

Memory is a complicated thing, a relative to truth, but not its twin.

—Barbara Kingsolver, 1990

If contemporary newspapers are the first draft of history, then oral histories and traditions should be considered the second draft. Like the articles that appear in daily or weekly newspapers, they convey important information, but they also get some things wrong. Each source must be weighed against other sources when attempting to reconstruct the past. Their shortcomings must be admitted and supplemented where possible.

Oral traditions within local communities transmit valuable information about other times, but they are often imprecise in dates and convey more of a period's flavor through anecdotes than a precise rebuilding of events. Historians should and do rely on a wide array of sources in reconstructing the past, and oral history can add vivacity and color to the basic details of a life, a community, or a period of time. Historians also recognize the tendency among informants to confuse or telescope chronology and to conflate events. Although such recorded memories present problems of verification, reminiscences remain valuable historical sources.[1]

The first oral historian to gather information on Abraham Lincoln was his third and final law partner, William H. Herndon. Shortly after Lincoln's death, Herndon began collecting reminiscences of people's memories of his martyred friend and partner, both through letters and personal interviews. Herndon sold copies of many of these notes to fellow Illinois attorney Ward Hill Lamon, who, with the writing assistance of Chauncey Black, produced a biography of his friend Abraham Lincoln in 1872. Herndon's interviews contributed significantly to the influential biography he wrote with Jesse Weik and published in 1889. Every substantial biography of Lincoln since these early ones by his contemporaries and friends has made extensive use of reminiscent material from Herndon and others, especially for Lincoln's pre-presidential years.² Perhaps it was a brief meeting that Herndon had with twenty-four-year-old George W. Smith that inspired the latter to collect reminiscences and oral traditions about Lincoln and southern Illinois, which contribute so much to When Lincoln Came to Egypt.³

* * *

The land called "Egypt" was important to Lincoln, for at different times in his political career, he had opportunities to venture there and encounter a culture—and an electorate—far different from those he knew in Sangamon County and central Illinois. With an imprecise northern border stretching from St. Louis, Missouri, in the west to Vincennes, Indiana, in the east, the area is bounded by two great rivers, the Ohio and the Mississippi, and comes to a point at Cairo. Like the land of Egypt in the Bible, southern Illinois' Egypt sent grain to help feed settlers in northern Illinois in the lean times of the 1830s.

In this area, as in biblical Egypt, slavery played a role. Some slaves worked in the saltworks in the eastern part of the region, while southern slave owners on their way to Missouri crossed the region with their slaves. A few Kentucky slave owners even brought their slaves to work Illinois lands but returned them each year to keep alive the legal fiction that they were merely "in transit" across the free state of Illinois.

The southern third of Illinois was the destination for so many migrants from the hills and valleys of the upper South that an

FOREWORD

identifiable Upland South cultural region developed there by 1850. This cultural region affected agricultural practices, economic strategies, religious beliefs, architecture, dialect, and foodways.[4]

It also affected political affiliation. Throughout Lincoln's life, southern Illinois was staunchly Democratic, as was much of the state. In the 1840s and 1850s, however, increased immigration to northern Illinois from New England and mid-Atlantic states brought more Whigs, then Republicans to the northern reaches of the state. By the time Lincoln was campaigning for statewide or national office, northern Illinois was a stronghold for the Republican Party, while southern Illinois remained firmly Democratic. The center of the state, where Lincoln had lived and practiced law for more than two decades, was more closely divided between the two major parties.[5]

Lincoln's major forays into Egypt for political purposes came in 1840, 1856, and 1858. In 1840, thirty-one-year-old Lincoln campaigned for as much as three months in southern Illinois on behalf of General William Henry Harrison as the Whig candidate for president. Although Harrison won the popular vote and garnered an electoral landslide nationwide, he lost Illinois and its five electoral votes. In Egypt, Harrison barely edged by Democratic incumbent Martin Van Buren in a handful of counties along the Ohio and Wabash Rivers, polling strongest in Wabash County among those in Egypt.

Lincoln's next campaigning voyages to Egypt were brief visits to towns on the northern periphery of the region, such as Belleville, Vandalia, Olney, and Albion in the autumn of 1856, when he was campaigning for Republican presidential candidate John C. Frémont. Egypt voted more overwhelmingly for Democratic candidate James Buchanan than it had for Van Buren sixteen years earlier.

Lincoln's final and perhaps most significant political travel in Egypt was during the course of his famed 1858 campaign against Stephen A. Douglas to represent Illinois in the U.S. Senate. The third of the Lincoln-Douglas debates took place in the heart of Egypt, in Jonesboro on September 15. One month later, the seventh and final debate occurred in Alton, along the vague northern

xiii

border of the region. At the election in November, Democratic candidates for the legislature won all the counties in Egypt, except St. Clair, Bond, and Edwards. In contrast to the Republican-dominated northern third of the state and the more divided center, southern Illinois steadfastly supported the Democratic candidates and rejected Lincoln and the Republicans.

These largely unsuccessful journeys into a politically hostile environment were perhaps instructive to Lincoln. Although he made little political headway, he did have friends in the region, though they were clearly in the political minority. So what did he learn from these political experiences?

Perhaps he drew the wrong lessons, for during the secession winter of 1860–61, President-elect Lincoln and many other Republicans consistently overestimated the extent of southern Unionism and underestimated the depth of Confederate resolve. Perhaps his friends in Egypt and even his political opponents had led him to believe that most southerners were devoted to the Union. Generally, southern Illinoisans were loyal, but they did not accurately represent the South of 1860.[6] And the war came.

* * *

George W. Smith, born in Greene County in 1855, was a lifelong resident of Illinois. As a young child during the Civil War, he had older brothers who fought for the Union. For two years in the 1870s, he attended Blackburn College in Carlinville, and taught in and superintended public schools for the next thirteen years. Although born and reared just a bit north of Egypt's boundary, he settled in Carbondale, the center of that region, in 1890, and remained there for the next fifty-five years. He went to Carbondale to become the principal of the training school at Southern Illinois Normal University. Seven years later, he became chair of the university's department of history and geography, a position he held until his retirement in 1935.

During his career, Smith first published A Student's History of Illinois *in 1906 and revised it several times afterward. He authored the three-volume* A History of Southern Illinois,

published in 1912, and the six-volume History of Illinois and
Her People, *published in 1927.* When Lincoln Came to Egypt
*(1940) was his last book. He was a member of the Illinois State
Historical Society for more than forty years and served as its vice
president for many years. He died at his home in Carbondale on
November 20, 1945.*[7]

Notes

1. Jan Vansina, *Oral Tradition: A Study in Historical Methodology* (Chicago: Aldine Publishing, 1965); Jan Vansina, *Oral Tradition as History* (Madison: University of Wisconsin Press, 1985); Barbara Allen
and William Lynwood Montell, *From Memory to History: Using Oral
Sources in Local Historical Research* (Nashville, TN: American Association for State and Local History, 1981), 20–22, 67–87.

2. William H. Herndon and Jesse W. Weik, *Herndon's Lincoln: The
True Story of a Great Life,* 3 vols. (Chicago: Belford, Clarke, 1889;
repr., Urbana: University of Illinois Press, 2006); Ward Hill Lamon, *The Life of Abraham Lincoln from His Birth to His Inauguration
as President* (Boston: James R. Osgood, 1872); Douglas L. Wilson
and Rodney O. Davis, eds., *Herndon's Informants: Letters, Interviews,
and Statement about Abraham Lincoln* (Urbana: University of Illinois Press, 1998), xlll–xxlv.

3. George W. Smith to David Donald, 15 November 1944, in David
Donald, *Lincoln's Herndon* (New York: Knopf, 1948), 286–87;
G. W. Smith, "Egypt's Cultural Contribution," in *Papers in Illi-
nois History and Transactions for the Year 1940* (Springfield: Illinois
State Historical Society, 1941), 48–49.

4. Douglas K. Meyer, *Making the Heartland Quilt: A Geographical History of Settlement and Migration in Early-Nineteenth-Century Illinois*
(Carbondale: Southern Illinois University Press, 2000), 136–68.

5. James L. Huston, "The Illinois Political Realignment of 1844–
1860: Revisiting the Analysis," *Journal of the Civil War Era* 1 (December 2011), 509–10.

6. Ed Gleeson, *Illinois Rebels: A Civil War Unit History of G Company,
15th Tennessee Regiment Volunteer Infantry* (Carmel: Guild Press of

Indiana, 1996). Lincoln, however, was not completely mistaken about southern Unionism. See Richard Nelson Current, *Lincoln's Loyalists: Union Soldiers from the Confederacy* (Boston: Northeastern University Press, 1992), and Daniel W. Crofts, *Reluctant Confederates: Upper South Unionists in the Secession Crisis* (Chapel Hill: University of North Carolina Press, 1989), 9–10.

7. George Washington Smith, *A Student's History of Illinois* (Bloomington, IL: Pantagraph Printing and Stationery, 1906); George Washington Smith, *A History of Southern Illinois: A Narrative Account of Its Historical Progress, Its People, and Its Principal Interests*, 3 vols. (Chicago: Lewis Publishing, 1912), 3:1714–17; George Washington Smith, *History of Illinois and Her People*, 6 vols. (Chicago: American Historical Society, 1927), 6:430–32; "News and Comment," *Journal of the Illinois State Historical Society* 38 (December 1945), 507–8.

INTRODUCTION

"Egypt," let it be said for the benefit of the uninitiated, is the southernmost part of Illinois. Theoretically, its north-ern boundary is an east-and-west line between St. Louis and Vincennes, Indiana, but in practice no strict adherence to this limit is enforced. Nevertheless, Egypt is a region with a sufficient number of common characteristics to give it a high degree of homogeneity. Its population is largely southern in origin. Except for occasional settlements, fewer European immigrant stocks are represented there than in other parts of the state. The towns are smaller, and the people live closer to the land. Most noticeable of all, to an outsider at least, is a staunch local patriotism. Those who live there are proud of Egypt—proud of her great coal and oil resources, of her rugged hills and lovely orchards, of her broad rivers and quiet towns. But deepest of all is their pride in her past. Egypt was a settled region long before the Indian yielded the northern part of Illinois to the white man, and many of the state's most prominent early citizens were her own sons.

Egyptians know and cherish the history of Southern Illinois, but elsewhere it has been largely disregarded. Even close students of Lincoln's life, for example, are inclined to think of him principally as a resident of New Salem and Springfield, or, if they extend the conception, as one whose

INTRODUCTION

absences from home took him over a judicial circuit in the central part of the state, and occasionally to Chicago. Yet Mr. Smith has shown that Lincoln was in Egypt on numerous occasions, and that he had many personal, professional and political friends in that section.

We are coming to recognize that Lincoln, like every other human being, cannot be understood apart from his environment—that to some extent at least he became the kind of man he was because of the surroundings in which he lived. Therein lies the importance of WHEN LINCOLN CAME TO EGYPT. *By adding detail to the bare record of Lincoln's visits to Egypt, by giving life to his friends there, by supplying long-neglected emphasis, George W. Smith, dean of the state's historians, has helped to complete the picture of the Illinois of Lincoln's time, and thus the picture of Lincoln himself. Students of Lincoln, students of Illinois, are permanently in his debt.*

PAUL M. ANGLE

AUTHOR'S PREFACE

The American people are fast forgetting that Abraham Lincoln was a Whig or a Republican. Neither do they care about his sectarian leanings. His life is becoming less and less mythical and more and more mysterious. Some people believe that Lincoln's special mission in the world was to direct the forces of right in the preservation of the government of the United States in the great crisis of the Civil War.

Surely in the middle part of the last century there was great need of wise leadership. An awful scourge—human slavery—had been morally and legally sustained within a limited area of our territory for two and a half centuries. But as the nation's population increased and popular government expanded, the awful scourge seemed more and more to strengthen its strangle hold upon the American people.

In the first serious contest between human freedom and human slavery, freedom was obliged to compromise, and the progress of the scourge was only temporarily checked. The public mind and the public conscience must continue to struggle with the problem of human slavery. Would it ever abate? The question of human slavery became involved in our political and in our religious life. As a result some of our large religious organizations were severed in twain, and only in recent years has there come a rapprochement.

It was however in our political life that the greatest danger to our peace and safety was found. In the early years of the period, the cause of human slavery was championed by a well organized political party. Opposition to slavery was increasing, but other political parties gave the cause of freedom indifferent support. There was a sad lack of efficient leadership, and the slave power and the extension of slave territory grew through war, through legislation, and through judicial decisions of the highest court in the land.

In the later years of this struggle over slavery and the extension of slave territory, there arose a man as by divine appointment who announced, by the authority of holy writ, "A house divided against itself cannot stand." It was this man of whom it was said, at his death, "Now he belongs to the ages." It was in the Court of the Cabildo in New Orleans that he heard the voice, "Whom shall I send, and who will go for us?" And he said, "Here am I, send me."

Lincoln returned to Illinois and while other great and good men organized opposition to the spread of slavery, Lincoln became the acknowledged leader of the forces that eventually abolished slavery. From the day that strong men wept as he delivered the "Lost Speech," in the Republican convention in 1856, to the day of his death, men stood in awe of his intellectual and moral power. Few men seemed to understand his mission in the world—this tall, gaunt, sad rail-splitter of the Sangamon, this tired man in the bedrab-bled linen duster who stood before his audience in Jones-boro and said before his opponent, Senator Douglas, "Why I know this people better than he does. I was raised just a little east of here. I am one of this people."

Long before he bade good-bye to the people of Spring-field in February, 1861, he was known as the protector of the oppressed, the defender of the defenseless. His friends loved to see him go, but were sad at his departure. The love of 1861 has never grown less. With such universal regard are Lincoln's rugged virtues esteemed that his comings and his goings in the central and the northern parts of the state have been carefully marked out. Roads, towns, hotels, bedrooms, chairs, and tables in any way related to his very active life, have been preserved and are to this day prized very highly.

Only lately have his personal relations to the people and places in Egypt become matters of general interest. In the pages following it is shown that Lincoln was closely related to the people of Southern Illinois. The farmers of Egypt whom Horace White observed coming into Jonesboro on the day of the debate, in ox wagons, the family sitting in home-made chairs, were in racial lineage closely allied to the homely man who with his friend walked the dusty path by the side of the road from the village square to the fairgrounds in Jonesboro the afternoon of September 15, 1858. Both the farmers and the homely man came from Virginia ancestry— one by way of Kentucky and Gentryville, Indiana, to the Sangamon country in Illinois; the others by way of Tennessee or Kentucky to the Egyptian Ozarks.

Nor were the cause of slavery and the extension of its territory without a directing genius, though this leadership was not always as wholehearted and as constant as was desirable, and near the end of the long struggle this leadership was spurned and repudiated.

Egypt, as the far down state of Illinois was called, was honored by the presence of the two great men, Lincoln and Douglas, who championed the opposing views as to the perpetuation and the extension of human slavery. Their joint visit to Egypt was of short duration and the facts and traditions relating thereto should be preserved and cherished. To accomplish in some measure this desirable end is the aim of this little volume.

> On a sloping hillside,
> In a grove of native trees,
> At the northern edge of a small county seat
> Nestling among the rugged Ozarks,
> Stands a small monument
> Marking the nearing of the end
> Of human slavery under the Stars and Stripes.
> —The Author.

THOSE WHO HAVE HELPED

Many friends here in Illinois have helped to gather the Lincoln facts that appear in the pages of this small volume. The author wishes in this way to express his thanks, and to acknowledge his indebtedness for their assistance in this labor of love:

MR. W. N. MOYER, *Historian*, MOUND CITY; MRS. JULIUS P. SCHUH, *D. A. R.*, CAIRO; MR. J. T. HUECKEL, *Manufacturer*, BELLEVILLE; MR. C. E. KANE, *Editor I. C. Railroad Magazine*, CHICAGO; MISS HALENE STREET, *Teacher*, BELLEVILLE; JUDGE WILLIAM T. PACE, MT. VERNON; MRS. RUTH B. BURCKHALTER, *Illinois Federation Women's Clubs*, ROBINSON; MRS. BESS EHRMANN, *Historian*, ROCKPORT, INDIANA; MRS. H. P. MARCHILDON, *Housewife*, THEBES; DR. LOUIS A. WARREN, *Historian*, FORT WAYNE, INDIANA; MR. JOHN SNYDER, *Former County Superintendent of Schools*, CAIRO; MR. GEORGE PARSONS, *Former Mayor*, CAIRO; MR. JAMES TAYLOR, MORGANFIELD, KENTUCKY; MRS. GRACE CABOT TOLER, *Editor*, MOUNDS; MR. O. W. METCALF, *Editor*, MT. VERNON; JUDGE J. V. HEIDINGER, FAIRFIELD; MRS. J. W. MAFFIT, *Historian*, CARMI; MISS MAUD UNDERWOOD, *Assistant Librarian*, BELLEVILLE; MR. C. L. KENNER, MT. CARMEL; MISS MARY JANE STEWART, *D. A. R.*, CARMI; DR. ANDY HALL, MT. VERNON; MR. CHARLES O. OTRICH, *Former County Superintendent of Schools*, JONESBORO; JUDGE THOMAS J. LAYMAN, BENTON; MR. TILLMAN MANUS, *Civil War Veteran*, ANNA; MR. GORDON MURPHEY, *Attorney*, CEN-

THOSE WHO HAVE HELPED

TRALIA; MR. WILLIAM C. CARSON, *Editor*, GREENVILLE; MISS MINNIE M. MCNEILL, *Teacher*, GREENVILLE; MRS. C. E. TRUESDAIL, *Hotel Proprietor*, CARLYLE; MR. J. M. HOWLEY, *Attorney*, CAIRO; MR. W. W. WILLIAMS, *B. and O. S. W. Railway Agent*, CAIRO; MRS. OSCAR L. HERBERT, *D. A. R.* CAIRO; MR. WILL TOLER, *Business Manager*, MOUNDS; MR. ANDREW JACKSON BUNCH, *Blacksmith*, MCCLURE; MR. C. E. TRUESDAIL, *Hotel Proprietor*, CARLYLE; MR. JOHN P. REESE, *Civil War Veteran*, COBDEN; MRS. HENRY HACKER, JONESBORO; MR. J. L. HACKER, *Retired Steamboat Captain*, CAIRO; MR. HORACE WHITE, *Former Editor, Chicago Tribune*, CHICAGO; MRS. FANNY P. HACKER, *Former County Superintendent of Schools*, CAIRO; MR. JOSEPH L. BARTLEY, *Attorney*, SHAWNEETOWN; MRS. CHARLES E. DAVIDSON, *National Society D. A. R.*, GREENVILLE; MR. E. L. DUKES, *Historian*, ALBION; MR. JOE W. RICKERT, *Attorney*, WATERLOO; MRS. ANNA FRANKLAND, ALBION; MRS. MARY JENNINGS, *Librarian*, THEBES; MR. W. T. WOODEN, MT. VERNON; MR. H. C. VORIS, *Editor*, WATERLOO; MR. FRANK LACKEY, *Merchant*, VILLA RIDGE; MRS. CHARLES CARROLL, CHICAGO; MISS ANNA FRANKLAND, *Secretary Historical Society*, ALBION; MRS. MYRA E. WIEDERHOLD, *Merchant*, SHAWNEETOWN; MR. NAT SMITH, *Former State Senator*, ALBION; MISS KATE BOWMAN, ALBION; MR. E. G. LENTZ, *Dean of Men, Teachers College*, CARBONDALE; MRS. JAMES W. TWITCHELL, *D. A. R.*, BELLEVILLE; DR. S. E. PARK, *1817 Church St.*, EVANSTON; MR. HARRY PRATT, *Secretary Lincoln Association*, SPRINGFIELD; MR. T. P. HANNA, *Attorney*, FAIRFIELD; MR. PAUL B. COUSLEY, *Editor*, ALTON; MISS HELEN MACMACKIN, *State Regent, Daughters of the American Revolution*, SALEM; MR. CLYDE HENSON, *High School History Teacher*, SALEM.

WHEN LINCOLN CAME TO EGYPT

WHENCE CAME THE EGYPTIANS

Before the battle of Yorktown, the last major engagement of the revolutionary struggle, thousands of rugged
pioneers from the states of Virginia, the Carolinas, and
Georgia had moved over the mountains. Here they founded
homes, and organized life in scores of places in the territory
south of the Ohio river. These pioneer men and women
brought with them over the mountains strong bodies, physical
courage, the love of home, and a touch of the old plantation
life.

In addition to the rugged virtues of their early colonial
life, these southern pioneers brought with them two serious
handicaps—human slavery and an indifference toward free,
popular education. These two handicaps lingered long in
the states west of the southern Alleghanies.

Among the pioneers who came out of Old Virginia
and settled in Kentucky, were the ancestors of Abraham
Lincoln—Honest Abe—long a household word in millions
of homes in the United States.

The territory north of the Ohio river, before the days
of the Revolution, had been the possessions of Massachusetts,
Connecticut, and Virginia. But these states had ceded their
claims to this land to the general government, and it in turn
had enacted the Ordinance of 1787 for the government of
the people when they should settle in this region.

In the winter of 1787-88, a band of forty-eight New
England Puritans made the journey overland to the junction
of the Muskingum river with the Ohio, and there founded

1

the city of Marietta, Ohio, the first American settlement
west of Pennsylvania and north of the Ohio river.

These forty-eight New England pioneers were basically
of the same stock as the pioneers who came into the regions
to the south of the Ohio, and like them these New England
Puritans brought over the mountains with them strong
bodies, physical courage, and the love of their New England
firesides. But unlike their brethren to the south of the Ohio,
instead of the handicaps of slavery and an indifference
toward education, these New England pioneers brought deep
convictions concerning free labor and free, popular education.

There were in the period of the American revolution,
far-seeing statesmen who were willing to risk their lives,
their fortunes, and their sacred honor in the cause of American Independence. One man stands far out in front, without whose genius in political theory and practical organization, the Northwest Territory would never have reached
her present status in human progress. This man was Thomas
Jefferson who, geographically, belonged with the slave-
holding south, yet the many years of his political thought
and activity seem to have borne their richest fruitage in the
institutional life of the Old Northwest. Education and
human freedom were guaranteed in the Ordinance of 1787.
"Religion, morality, and knowledge being necessary to good
government and the happiness of mankind, schools and the
means of education shall be forever encouraged." It further
provided: "There shall be neither slavery nor involuntary
servitude in the said territory, otherwise than for the punishment of crimes whereof the party shall have been convicted." Thomas Jefferson did not write these words, but
he was the father of these great principles.

Our New England forefathers brought into this new
West well defined notions and permanently fixed beliefs in
popular government, industry, education, morality, and religion. These fundamentals were reinforced by the doctrines
of social justice, an intelligent democracy, civil rights, and

2

human freedom as enumerated by Thomas Jefferson. Thus was blended in the pioneer life of the Old Northwest, as we shall see, all that was best in the life of the New England *Puritan* and in the life of the Southern *Cavalier*.

In the closing decade of the eighteenth century and the first quarter of the nineteenth, thousands of pioneers from New England and from the Middle Atlantic states made their way over the mountains and down the beautiful Ohio, to settle in the thriving villages, towns, and cities then growing up along the north side of the Ohio's inviting shores. Not only so, but thousands of others ventured out into the interior of the Northwest and became the first settlers of Ohio, Indiana, and Illinois.

It should be remembered that what is now Illinois was slave territory when France claimed it, and also when Great Britain owned it. When this territory came into the possession of the United States by the treaty of 1783, this government guaranteed to British subjects living within the limits of the region north of the Ohio, the right of ownership of their property—which guaranteed to them the ownership of their slaves. And although the Ordinance of 1787 forbade slavery, the courts held that those slaves already held in Illinois could still be legally held, as well as their offspring, but that slaves brought into Illinois for permanent residence were free by the Ordinance of 1787. Notwithstanding these facts, there were hundreds and even thousands of pioneers opposed to slavery who established their homes in the land of Egypt, as Southern Illinois was then being called. They believed that eventually slavery would be driven from the entire Northwest territory.

Whence came the forty thousand people whose presence in Egypt in 1818 justified the admission of Illinois into the Union as a state? Let us look a little more carefully into their immediate origin. When Marietta, Ohio, was settled in 1788, there were in the territory which afterwards became the state of Illinois, only fifty adult Americans. These half hundred Americans lived in and about the French vil-

WHEN LINCOLN CAME TO EGYPT

lages of Cahokia, St. Phillip, St. Ann, Prairie du Rocher, and Kaskaskia. These French villagers and the fifty Americans who lived among them may very properly be considered the first group of pioneers in the settlement of Illinois.

The second group consisted of a few score of the soldiers who had marched across Southern Illinois with Colonel George Rogers Clark in two historic campaigns in the conquest of the Northwest Territory in 1778-79. They were of good stock, but few in number, and were largely from Virginia and Kentucky, though other states furnished a part of the small band. These "Virginia Long Knives" had been attracted by the mild winter of 1778-79, the fertile soil, the perpetual water supply in springs and small streams, the abundant forests, and the great variety of wild life. The presence of a few negro slaves did not outweigh the many good qualities of the country. Most of this group came before the end of the 18th century, and settled near the French villages.

The third group of pioneers who swelled the growing numbers came directly from Kentucky and Tennessee. These two were the first states to be admitted into the Union from the territory west of the Alleghanies; Kentucky was admitted in 1792, and Tennessee in 1796. Most of the people who lived in these two states at the end of the 18th century were originally from the states east of the mountains. Not a large number was native born. Many of the people from the coast states were restless, adventurous. They did not stay long in Kentucky and Tennessee, but sought new lands to conquer in the Old Northwest. It has been estimated that considerably more than fifty per cent of the adult population in Illinois in 1818 was from the regions south of the Mason and Dixon line and the Ohio river. This fact gave to Egypt, as this region was soon to be known, the make-up of a southern state.

The ancestors of Abraham Lincoln, as is well known, were English immigrants who came to Massachusetts in the early part of the 17th century. The descendants of one,

4

WHEN LINCOLN CAME TO EGYPT

Samuel, migrated through New Jersey, Pennsylvania, Virginia, Kentucky, Indiana, to the Sangamon country in central Illinois. In like manner many thousands of immigrants came, after short residences along the way, from the Atlantic coast to Southern Illinois.

The fourth group consisted of a goodly number of sturdy men and women from the "old thirteen" who had been attracted to the territory afterward made into the state of Missouri, by the cry for more men to labor in the salt works and in the lead and iron mines and furnaces of the Ozarks. These people had lived in Missouri only a few years, but they prospered and with their earnings many sought cheap lands, and homes in what they thought soon would be a new state. Dr. John Logan, father of General John A. Logan, though coming a little later, represents this movement. They were probably about evenly divided as to the slavery issue.

A fifth group, though small in numbers, furnished settlers in many localities. These were known as the "Pennsylvania Dutch." They were chiefly farmers, very earnest and thrifty. They were great lovers of freedom and made admirable citizens. They were not clannish and yet they were usually found in small numbers or groups in localities where they settled. They readily adapted themselves to the prevailing social and economic conditions wherever they settled. Dr. Conrad Will, who settled on Big Muddy river, was a fine example of this group. He not only practiced his profession, but manufactured salt, kept an inn, sat in the Illinois constitutional convention of 1818, and afterwards in the legislature.

The sixth group and the previous group probably should be studied together. They were of the same stock. Prior to 1818 a few Germans direct from the Fatherland came into Egypt. These early arrivals opened the way for the coming of many hundreds of their kindred. They settled chiefly in what later came to be St. Clair and neighboring counties. They were for a free state in the struggle of 1824.

WHEN LINCOLN CAME TO EGYPT

The seventh group of Illinois pioneers came direct from England. They settled in what is now Edwards county. Morris Birkbeck and George Flower, two commoners, men of education, wealth, and culture led this colony. The motives which brought them to America and to Illinois were to escape from political tyranny, and religious and economic oppression; and the attraction of cheap lands, free soil, democracy, and nature's abundant provision in soil, timber, water, and climate. The leaders believed Illinois would eventually be a free state, and the probability that each one could easily become the owner of a homestead made it a simple task to gather immigrants from the over-crowded conditions in England.

Birkbeck and Flower and many of their followers were apostles of the higher life. They exemplified in their daily living the highest ideals of industry, thrift, temperance, freedom of thought, and liberty of action. One of the purposes of these people was to work out a type of communistic society in a locality where there would be few distractions from groups who had other ideals. Two towns or centers were established in Edwards county—Albion, which was known as Flower's town, and Wanborough which was known as Birkbeck's town. The influence of the English settlements in Edwards county has been far reaching. The people of Illinois are coming more and more to appreciate the higher standards of life which these pioneers set up for the common people in this wilderness country.

The coming of these several groups was a continuing process. These nuclei of early settlements were continually expanding in numbers and growing in complexity in their every day life. The population of Illinois in 1790 was sixty-five American families or about 325 souls; in 1810 the number had increased to 12,284; and in 1818 the census enumerators reported a population of 40,000. In 1818 the people were looking forward to statehood.

In that same year statehood was granted and the constitution for the new state was accepted. The clause in that

6

document which concerns us in this study of Illinois, originally read: "There shall be neither slavery nor involuntary servitude in this state otherwise than for the punishment of crimes whereof the party shall have been duly convicted." This was in conformity with the wording and the spirit of the Ordinance of 1787. But this clause would have freed every negro slave in Illinois which had been held over from the old French regime and the English ownership of the Northwest Territory, had not the Council of Revision, a committee of the constitutional convention of 1818, brought in a new article pertaining to slavery which read, "Neither slavery nor involuntary servitude shall hereafter be introduced into this State, otherwise than for the punishment of crimes whereof the party shall have been duly convicted." This change in Article VI of the Constitution reveals the fact that the majority of the delegates was in favor of retaining slavery as it then existed in Illinois, but was opposed to opening the doors to any further introduction of that "peculiar institution."

Now certain groups of Illinois pioneers we have described were opponents of slavery. It will therefore not be a surprise to find that slavery was one of the subjects of general discussion. It became a matter of serious discussion at the inauguration of Edward Coles, the second governor of the state. Governor Coles was a disciple of Thomas Jefferson and a bitter opponent of slavery, which interests attempted to make Illinois a slave state by rewriting its constitution. The conflict lasted two years. The cause of slavery was defeated and did not disturb the public mind again until toward the middle of the century.

LINCOLN MEMORIAL ON ILLINOIS SIDE OF WABASH OPPOSITE
VINCENNES, INDIANA.

LINCOLN IN PUBLIC LIFE

Abraham Lincoln came into public life in the summer of 1832, at the age of twenty-three. He was summoned to duty as a militiaman April 16, 1832, on the occasion of the Black Hawk war. Lincoln was at that time an announced candidate for the legislature at the election the first Monday in August of that year. He was discharged from his third and last enlistment at Whitewater, Wisconsin, July 10, 1832. When he arrived at New Salem in mid-summer, he renewed his campaigning for the legislature. And though it would seem that his military service should have been some help in the canvass, it evidently did not for he was defeated.

In this campaign Lincoln ran as an avowed Clay man though it was generally known that he was a Whig. Judge Stephen T. Logan, in speaking of Lincoln's candidacy for the legislature in 1832 said, "The Democrats of New Salem worked for Lincoln out of their personal regard for him. He was as stiff as a man could be in his Whig doctrines. They did this simply because he was popular, because he was Lincoln." Judge Logan states definitely that Lincoln was a Whig as early as 1832.

The Whig party came into being as a protest against the theories of the Democratic party as interpreted by Jackson and Van Buren. The Whigs were from the beginning a party of opposition, but as the fourth decade rolled along, the leaders stated more definitely a few constructive policies. By 1840 the Whig party supported a national banking system, a protective tariff, internal improvements, and

9

opposed the "spoils system." The national leaders were supported by local leaders in the several states.

Lincoln's defeat in 1832 may have been a blessing in
disguise. In the short two years, from 1832 to 1834, he had
been active in several callings which had thrown him in contact with a large number of new people. He had thus en-
larged his acquaintance and strengthened his friendships.
Miss Tarbell says, "He was conscious of his popularity." At
any rate he was a candidate for the legislature again in 1834,
and this time he was successful. The capital had been moved
in 1820 from Kaskaskia to Vandalia, yet it was still a long
journey from Salem to Vandalia.

The ninth session of the legislature met the first Monday in December, 1834. Lincoln took his seat in that session
with Edwin B. Webb of White county, Jesse K. Dubois of
Lawrence, John Dougherty of Union, Adam W. Snyder of
St. Clair, John S. Hacker of Union, William J. Gatewood
of Gallatin, William L. D. Ewing of Fayette, John T. Stuart
of Sangamon, and James Semple of Madison, most of them
Egyptians. Though only twenty-five years old, possessing
little contact with public men, and affiliated with the minority party in Illinois and in the nation, Lincoln soon took
high rank as a valuable member of the legislature.

It was here that Lincoln met Mr. Douglas, then barely
twenty-one years old and who was an applicant for appointment as prosecuting attorney in the first judicial district. His
rival for appointment was John J. Hardin, a brilliant lawyer
from Jacksonville. Douglas secured the appointment. From
this first meeting, Lincoln and Douglas remained good
friends.

Lincoln was elected to the tenth general assembly which
met in December, 1836. The center of population in Illinois
was rapidly moving northward in the state and there seemed
some good reason that the state's capital should also move
in that direction. Springfield and Sangamon county, then
the center of a rich farming region and of a rapidly increasing population, was sending nine members to the legislature.

WHEN LINCOLN CAME TO EGYPT

Eight of these assemblymen chose Lincoln to lead the forces to secure the location of the capital in Springfield. In such high esteem was this tall rail-splitter from the Sangamon held, and so skillfully did he direct his campaign, that the "Long Nine" won the battle and Springfield became the state's new capital. Substantial help in the contest came from Egyptian friends whom Lincoln never forgot.

Lincoln served four terms in the legislature and refused to serve longer as he wished to lay plans for a congressional career. Douglas had risen rapidly in public favor. From prosecuting attorney in the first judicial district, he had held the office of Register of the Land Office, had served in the legislature, sat on the Supreme Court, and been in congress from 1843 to 1847. In the meantime Lincoln had become known as a good lawyer, and was regarded as being a great public speaker and shrewd debator. Douglas was known as a Democrat and Mr. Lincoln was a Whig.

Lincoln was the Whig candidate for congress in the fall election of 1846. His opponent was the famous Reverend Peter Cartwright. Lincoln was elected. Congress met in December, 1847, and while Lincoln was taking the oath of office in the lower house, Douglas was sworn in as United States senator. In this congress Lincoln was a lone Whig with six Democrats from Illinois. This congress had to do with finishing up the Mexican war. Lincoln was very un-happy in congress, for he felt that the war was going to profit slavery in that the territory which the United States was acquiring would eventually become slave territory. He was not a candidate for re-election, but gave his whole time to his growing law practice. His office was in Springfield.

11

THE KANSAS-NEBRASKA BILL

By the middle of the century the great national political leaders who had guided party organizations were passing from their labors. Jackson, Clay, Crawford, Webster, Calhoun turned the ship of state over to far less experienced hands. The bitter feelings engendered by the slavery discussions had left the two old political parties—Democrats and Whigs—very much disorganized and new parties were in the offing.

In the discussions on the Compromise of 1850, there had come forward champions of two opposite veiws as to slavery. One group favored the popular sovereignty idea, the clause in the Compromise pertaining to Utah and New Mexico which stated that when these territories should be admitted as states, they should come in with or without slavery, as their constitutions may prescribe at the time of their admission." Douglas joined Clay in supporting this political doctrine. Seward of New York and Chase of Ohio joined against the popular sovereignty doctrine. Seward claimed there was a "higher law" than the constitution. Lincoln, while not in congress, agreed with Seward—and thus we see one of the basic features of the great Lincoln-Douglas Debate—moral law versus expediency.

Franklin Pierce was elected president in 1852, carrying all the states except Kentucky, Tennessee, Vermont, and Massachusetts. In his inaugural address in March, 1853, he said he was thankful for the quiet which prevailed in the land, and for the passing of a "perilous crisis," and further,

13

"that this respose is to suffer no shock during my official term, if I have the power to prevent it." It has been stated that early in his term he was closeted with Douglas and a group of Southern leaders in a conference out of which came the bill for the introduction of the Kansas-Nebraska law.

The unorganized territory left from the Louisiana Purchase after Missouri came into the union was known as Nebraska. Stephen A. Douglas had been chairman of the committee on territories for several terms. At the opening of the first congress in Pierce's term, December, 1853, a bill was introduced into the senate providing for the organization of the Nebraska territory. The bill was referred to Senator Douglas' committee. After considerable jockeying, a bill was reported out providing for two territories—Kansas and Nebraska. The bill was later amended. One amendment reading: "That all questions pertaining to slavery in the territories and in the new states to be formed therefrom, are to be left to the decision of the people residing therein, through their appropriate representatives."

Douglas argued that by the adoption of the Compromise of 1850 the people of the United States had endorsed the principle of "squatter sovereignty." But a careful student of the debates in the Compromise says: "There was no hint in the debates of 1850 that the Compromise measures were meant to apply to any other region than the territory just acquired in the Mexican war." Another writer says: "It was expansion, not slavery, that he (Douglas) was interested in, and if he incorporated the slavery clause in his Kansas-Nebraska Bill to make it palatable to the South, it was certainly not with the intention of extending slavery, and probably not primarily with the intention of gaining the presidency, but for the immediate object of getting the territory organized." Rhodes says: "The action of the Illinois senator was a bid for Southern support in the next Democratic convention." A friendly critic, however, holds: "He (Douglas) had no deep ethical convictions on the subject of slavery, for again and again he has said he didn't care

14

whether slavery was voted up or voted down."

On the day after the introduction of the Kansas-Nebraska bill, a group of Northern independent Democrats signed "The Appeal of the Independent Democrats." This appeal denounced the Kansas-Nebraska bill as "a gross viola-lation of a sacred pledge; part and parcel of an atrocious plot to exclude from a vast and unoccupied region immigrants from the Old World and free laborers from our own states, and to convert it into a region of despotism inhabited by masters and slaves." This appeal was signed by Senators Wade, Chase, Sumner, Everett, Seward, and others.

In the struggle for the passage of the Kansas-Nebraska bill, Douglas had valuable help, but he was the acknow-ledged leader. "For the measure, Douglas waged a brilliant fight upon the floor of the senate." He met with consummate skill in debate, the powerful arguments of Seward, Chase, and Sumner.

At midnight on the third of March, 1854, Douglas arose in the senate to close the long contest. As the morning light in the East was breaking, the debate ended, and in the solemn hush of a new day the roll was called. Thirty-seven senators voted "Yea" and fourteen voted "No;" and as the senate adjourned amid the booming of cannon, Douglas stood the unrivaled champion of popular sovereignty. The bill was rushed through the house under the leadership of another Illinoisan, William A. Richardson. It became a law May 30, 1854.

Everywhere now, except in the deep South, there was a breaking away from old political moorings. Whigs and northern Democrats were dividing and subdividing. We read of Free Soilers, Anti-Nebraska Democrats, Whigs, Democrats, Know-Nothings, and Republicans.

From the end of Lincoln's term in congress in March, 1849, to the passage of the Kansas-Nebraska bill in 1854, that amiable gentleman was absorbed in the study and prac-tice of his chosen profession. In these early days in Illinois, lawyers went far and near in their attendance upon the sittings of the courts. In fact, lawyers would usually follow the judge as he went from one county seat to another in his judicial circuit. It was in this way that Lincoln became so well known in the Eighth Judicial Circuit, a large territory in central Illinois including seventeen counties. Lincoln, in the years preceding the great debate, had been engaged in many great law cases, but the one that has come down to us as the really most important was one in which he was counsel for the Illinois Central Railroad Company. For his services in this case, he collected a fee of five thousand dollars.

THE BOWMAN HOTEL, ALBION, ILLINOIS.

RISE OF THE REPUBLICAN PARTY

In the months of bitter conflict in congress over the repeal of the Missouri Compromise, or the Kansas-Nebraska bill, there was a gradual drawing together of the opponents of the extension of slave territory. This was true not only in the congress of the United States, but back home in the northern states, among the people in cities, towns, villages, and even in rural communities. Through several local organizations designated by a variety of names, the unification was taking place. The appeal of the Independent Democrats was probably the first outspoken opposition to this legal support of the extension of slave territory.

As early as February 28, 1854, a small group of Wisconsin citizens met in a school house in Ripon, Wisconsin, and "recommended that a new party be organized on the issue of slavery extension." On July 6, 1854, at Jackson, Michigan, several thousand people met in a mass meeting and organized against the Kansas-Nebraska Act. This mass convention announced a platform and named Anti-Nebraska candidates for several offices who were successful in the fall elections. Opponents to the extension of slave territory in Ohio, Wisconsin, Vermont, and Massachusetts took steps to encourage the growth of Anti-Nebraska sentiment.

Illinois was rich soil for the growth of Anti-Nebraska sentiment, in spite of the fact that this state was the home of the champion of the Kansas-Nebraska Act, which meant the extension of slave territory. On October 3, 1854, Senator Douglas appeared in Springfield to set himself right be-

17

fore his friends who were attending the state fair. He had lately been over the state repairing his "broken fences." His Springfield speech delivered in Representative Hall on October 3, 1854, was a powerful defense of his position as leader in securing the repeal of the Missouri Compromise. He generously announced that he understood Lincoln would speak on the next day, October 4, which he did. Douglas listened to Lincoln on the afternoon of the fourth, and re' plied on the fifth. These three speeches in Springfield may be regarded as the first stages of the great debate.

Lincoln had now really taken his first step toward leadership in the Republican party. From this time forward he was jointly concerned with leaders in this new party in conferences and conventions. In the November election of 1854, Lincoln was elected to the legislature much against his wish. He resigned before the legislature met in January that he might be a candidate before that body for United States senator to succeed Senator Shields. The legislature could not easily decide and it appeared that neither Lincoln nor Trumbull would be chosen. Lincoln withdrew from the contest and Trumbull was elected.

A long step forward in the growth of the Republican party in Illinois was taken in the spring of 1856. This was the call of an Anti-Nebraska Editorial Convention to be held in Decatur, February 22. The avowed purpose was the making of arrangements for the organization of the Anti-Nebraska forces in Illinois. Twenty-five papers published in Illinois endorsed the movement. Southern Illinois sentiment may be discovered when we learn that the Belleville Advo' cate and the Sparta Journal were the only papers south of Springfield that endorsed this convention.

The convention met on the day appointed, but owing to a heavy snow storm on the evening and night before over central and northern Illinois, only fifteen of the twenty- five editors who signed the call reported at the meeting. The work of the convention was done mainly through commit' tees. The most important was the committee on resolutions

18

headed by Dr. Charles H. Ray, editor of The Chicago Tribune. A State Central Committee was appointed and authorized to call a state convention for the purpose of put' ting out an Anti-Nebraska ticket for state offices. On this committee, Joseph Gillespie of Edwardsville was named for the eighth congressional district and D. L. Phillips of Anna for the ninth. Lincoln was a visitor to this editorial conven' tion and it is presumed he assisted Dr. Ray in formulating the report of the committee on resolutions.

The State Central Committee called a state convention as requested, and at the appointed time, according to the records, 236 delegates reported. Twenty-five of the thirty- three Southern Illinois counties, usually called Egypt, were not represented in the Bloomington meeting. Of the eight counties in Egypt that sent delegates to the Bloomington meeting—namely, St. Clair, Union, Washington, Randolph, Marion, Madison, Edwards, and Bond—all voted against slavery in 1824 except Marion county.

This Bloomington gathering, though practically Repub' lican, was called as an Anti-Nebraska meeting. John M. Palmer, a Democrat, was made chairman. The work, largely done by committees, consisted in making a platform and naming candidates for state offices. Colonel William H. Bissell of St. Clair county was nominated for governor. Among the delegates who afterward came into prominence in Illinois were John M. Palmer, O. H. Browning, John Wentworth, Norman B. Judd, W. P. Kellogg, Richard Yates, I. L. Morrison, John G. Nicolay, O. M. Hatch, Wil' liam H. Herndon, and Abraham Lincoln. The Democratic convention was held early in May. It nominated for governor William A. Richardson, a loyal Douglas supporter.

The Democrats held their national convention at Cin' cinnati and put forward James Buchanan for the presidency. The newly organized Republican party met at Philadelphia in national convention and nominated John C. Fremont for that high office. The campaign was patterned after the "Tip' pecanoe" canvass of 1840, but carried on with less enthusiasm. Bissell was elected governor of Illinois and that party was successful in several other states, but Buchanan was elected president.

No particular day can be named as the birthday of the Republican party in Illinois. As early as 1854 the word Republican was used by groups who opposed the Kansas-Nebraska Act. The party in Illinois was made up of former Whigs and Anti-Nebraska Democrats.

KANSAS—SLAVE OR FREE

When the Kansas-Nebraska bill became a law on May 30, 1854, there was a vigorous movement of opposing forces into the rich lands of Kansas. The important question was—Shall Kansas be slave or free territory, and later a free or a slave state? By the doctrine of "squatter sovereignty" this was a question of numbers or majority, and since the majority was to decide the question, it was necessary for both sides to swell their numbers.

The slavery interests of the South were, for the time being, dependent upon the slave holders and slavery interest in western Missouri to go in and possess the land. This they could do because all the machinery of government was at their call. The anti-slavery interests were dependent upon real home-seekers who wanted to settle in free territory. These "Sons of the South" from Missouri were very temporary "squatters" for many of them had left wives and children back in Missouri.

Aid societies were organized in New England to help free settlers to reach Kansas overland. The first test vote was in the election of a territorial legislature. This occurred in 1855. The "Sons of the South" easily carried the election. A census taken by the governor showed 2,900 voters in the whole territory. But on election day 6,320 votes were cast. The town of Lawrence with 360 registered voters cast 781 votes. The first territorial legislature was therefore a pro-slavery body. The slave laws of Missouri were adopted. The free-state settlers organized a government of their own with

21

Topeka as the capital. The territory now had two state governments. The war began. Burnings and murder became the order of the day.

The pro-slavery interests of Kansas presented to congress a constitution and an application for admission into the union. The convention which made this constitution met at Lecompton and the document was therefore called the Lecompton Constitution. When the constitution was submitted, for adoption by the people, the question was, should Kansas be a state with limited or unlimited slavery? The free-state people refused to take part in adopting such a constitution, and the majority was for unlimited slavery; the vote for unlimited slavery was 6,143 to 589 against.

While this Kansas turmoil was at its height, the Supreme Court of the United States rendered a very famous decision on the Dred Scott case. Suffice it to say the decision implied that congress could not prevent a man from taking his property with him anywhere in the United States. Hence, neither territories nor states could legally exclude slavery.

Congress met December, 1857. Douglas, so far, had kept "hands off" with regard to the Kansas conflict. But he was as profoundly disgusted with the failure of the "squatter sovereignty" plan as were any of the anti-slavery leaders. He called on President Buchanan to consider the business of the coming session. He told the President it would never do to submit the Lecompton Constitution to congress. Douglas said it violated the plighted faith of the President and his party. The President said he must submit it, and recommend the admission of Kansas under the Lecompton Constitution. The President grew excited and said, "Mr. Douglas, I desire you to remember that no Democrat ever yet differed from an administration of his own choice without being crushed." Senator Douglas replied, "Mr. President, I wish to inform you that General Jackson is dead." From that hour there opened wider and wider a great gulf between Senator Douglas and the President, and also between the senator from Illinois and the slavery interests in the South.

WHEN LINCOLN CAME TO EGYPT

The President submitted the Lecompton Constitution to congress with a message urging its acceptance and the admission of Kansas under the Lecompton Constitution. The constitution and the message were referred to Senator Douglas' committee on territories. After wrestling with the matter for six days, the majority of the committee reported favorably and recommended the admission of Kansas under the Lecompton Constitution. Douglas and others presented a minority report and the debate then began in the senate.

March 22, 1858, was announced as the day when Douglas would speak on the admission of Kansas. He was just recovering from a fortnight's illness. The hour allotted him to speak was seven o'clock in the evening. Standing room in senate chamber, galleries, and in the halls was at a premium. The occasion was Douglas' Rubicon. Here he would completely break with the President and his advisers. He showed that congress was here asked to force upon the people of Kansas a constitution against their will and which was rejected on a recent vote of the people by 10,226 to 162. Douglas said the question at issue was not a party question, and he contended that the President had no right to tell a senator his duty and demand his allegiance. "If the will of my state is one way and the will of the President is the other, am I to be told that I must obey the executive and betray my state, or else be hounded as a traitor to the party and hunted down by all the newspapers that share the patronage of the government? And every man who holds a petty office in any part of my state to have the question put to him, are you Douglas' enemy? If not, your head comes off." The bill for admission passed the senate 33 to 25, but failed in the house.

Congress adjourned in the early midsummer, since the congressional elections were to occur that fall. One-third of the United States senators would also be elected by the legislatures chosen in the November election. Douglas was a

23

candidate to succeed himself. Lincoln was his opponent on the Republican ticket. Senator Douglas early expressed his respect for his opponent as a campaigner.

JOEL LACKEY HOME, PULASKI, ILLINOIS.

DOUGLAS TRIUMPHANT

The coming of Senator Douglas to Illinois in the summer of 1858 was in marked contrast with his return to the
state in 1854. In the earlier return to his adopted state and
to former friends and supporters, he was received by a raging
mob that refused to hear him speak and who by their actions
and expressions showed they had lost all respect for his
motives and confidence in his statesmanship. "A tide of
fanatical passion had set against him, not only in the Old
North, but in the New Northwest, the field of his former
undisputed mastery." And yet he returned in 1854 as the
winner of a great battle, the champion of a great contest.
William H. Seward said of him in 1854 at the close of the
Kansas-Nebraska debate, "I never had so much respect for
him as I have tonight."

But in 1858 when he returned as the champion defender of freedom in Kansas, as the object of Buchanan's
vindictive onslaught, as the challenger of the united interests
of the slave power, his coming was celebrated by the plaudits
of thousands who extended a royal welcome and renewed
their pledge of loyalty.

On the evening of July 9, 1858, he addressed the
thousands gathered in the streets, from the balcony of the
Tremont House, in Chicago. Lincoln was an attentive listener, and said the next evening, "I was furnished with a
seat very convenient for hearing him, and was otherwise
very courteously treated by him and his friends, and for
which I thank him and them." Douglas explained his action

25

in opposing the admission of Kansas under the Lecompton Constitution; he then took up a critical review of Lincoln's Springfield speech, "A house divided against itself."

The next evening from that same balcony, Lincoln answered Douglas. These two speeches in Chicago were allowed by Lincoln and Senator Douglas to be considered a "joint debate" in the second congressional district. On the 16th of July, Douglas addressed a vast throng in Bloomington, Illinois. Lincoln was again among his listeners. They went to Springfield together on the 17th, where Senator Douglas in the afternoon addressed an open-air meeting. That night Lincoln spoke in Representative Hall. These two speeches in Springfield were counted the second "joint debate," in the sixth congressional district.

While Douglas was in Springfield, he was in conference with the Democratic State Central Committee; they planned his speaking dates throughout the state, ending at Ottawa August 21. Lincoln and his advisers also planned a series of meetings. Following the second "joint debate" in Springfield, the newspapers supporting Senator Douglas complained that Lincoln was following Douglas around in order to get a hearing for himself before the Douglas audiences. "The Douglas papers made complaint that Lincoln was transgressing the ethics of campaigning by following their candidate and taking advantage of his crowds," says Sparks in Vol. III, Illinois Historical Collections. Douglas, it appears, was giving a good deal of attention in his speeches to Senator Trumbull, who had publicly made serious complaints against Douglas. Dr. Sparks says that Lincoln felt that Trumbull was getting too much free advertising, and in consultation with his friends, decided to challenge Douglas for a series of joint debates.

Lincoln addressed a very polite note to Senator Douglas on the 24th of July proposing a joint discussion from the same platform. Senator Douglas accepted. The details were very simple. There was to be one joint discussion in each of the nine congressional districts in Illinois except in the

second and the sixth. They had already held joint discussions in the second and sixth. The seven places designated
and the time were as follows:

Ottawa .... August 21
Freeport .... August 27
Jonesboro .... September 15
Charleston .... September 18
Galesburg .... October 7
Quincy .... October 13
Alton .... October 15

Both Lincoln and Douglas had speaking appointments
all along between any two of the above dates. These were
filled sometimes with difficulty on account of want of time
and the inconvenience of travel.

TWO GREAT LEADERS

In the years from 1830 to 1858 Illinois was a school of "hard knocks." Two ambitious young men were attending this school. They were destined to become Illinois' most distinguished citizens and the nation's greatest political leaders.

Illinois has always been a generous god-mother. The two ambitious young men were both immigrants—one from the rock-ribbed hills of Puritan New England; the other from the hilly slopes and valleys of the land of the Cavaliers. One had come from the land of spindles and looms, the other from the land of tobacco and cotton. One had passed through important cities, the marts of trade, on his way; the other through the forests and the three-faced log camps. One came light hearted and expectant, the other came carrying a great sorrow and apparently full of melancholy. One was a cabinet-maker before he came, the other was to be the nation's greatest *cabinet* maker. One began life in Illinois as a school teacher, the other as a rail-splitter.

Still these two young men had much in common. They were practically of the same age; they were both in their youth poor; they were both industrious; they were both good students; they were both good lawyers; they were both patriotic; the ending of each was sad and untimely.

In the earlier years of Douglas' career, it appeared that his life work would be in the line of the judiciary. It was thought that he was especially fitted for that phase of public service. But fate seemed to have selected for him a life of public service in the nation's legislative halls. And it was

WHEN LINCOLN CAME TO EGYPT

Clark E. Carr in a fine biography of Senator Douglas said: "In every one of those (seven) debates, Senator Douglas quoted the sentiment of Mr. Lincoln's speech, the house divided speech, and tried to answer it. The more he struggled to refute it, the more apparent did its truth appear."

The culmination of Lincoln's political leadership came in his election to the presidency in 1860.

SITE OF JONESBORO DEBATE.

THIS SECTION CALLED EGYPT

The importance of the junction of the Ohio river with the Mississippi, from a commercial point of view, was early and generally recognized. The French saw this importance as is shown by a concession, or charter, granted by the French government in 1702 to Sieur Charles Juchereau de St. Dennis to fortify the junction of the two rivers and to control all commercial transactions in the territory adjacent thereto. A fort, a tannery, and great warehouses were constructed on the banks of the Ohio just below the present Halliday Hotel in Cairo. But Juchereau and his band were driven out in 1705 by the Indians.

The English also saw in the region of the junction of the rivers great commercial opportunities. Early archeologists made comparisons between the alluvial areas of Southern Illinois and the great mounds found in them, and the Nile Valley and its great pyramids. Eastern American newspapers, and even British publications, stressed the commercial value of the region around the junction of the two mighty rivers.

It seems to have been easy for some early visitors to this locality to see the Nile delta in the extensive valleys of the Ohio and the Mississippi, and to see the pyramids in the great Kincaid and the Monks' mounds. From this stretch of the imagination, it was easy to call the region in Southern Illinois where these interesting features are found "Egypt." This name was applied even before the country was settled. Indeed, it could be shown that the common and continued use of the term was largely responsible for interest which centered about the junction of the two rivers in the early decades of the last century.

As early as 1818 it was proposed to establish an *entrepot* at or near the junction of the two rivers, bearing the name Cairo. Many years before Charles Dickens, the English novelist, saw Cairo in 1842, hundreds of thousands of pounds of English capital had been invested in commercial enterprises along the Illinois side of the lower Ohio river.

Southern Illinois was settled, as has been shown, by an agricultural people who were a sort of self-sufficing group. Many of them on coming into this region from the older southeastern states had settled in the hills and valleys of Egypt only after they had made a careful study of the rich prairies farther north around Springfield, Decatur, and Champaign.

In their study of these great prairies, they saw no way to conquer the tough prairie sod, or the cold of the long winters. They believed the drinking water of the flat prairies was a menace to good health, and they could not understand how there could ever be any social life where the homes were a mile or more apart. It was all repelling. In their imagination, they saw happiness in the simple log cabins on the hill-slopes of the Ozarks of Egypt. Here they would find an abundance of pure spring water, timbered shelters for their stock in the cold winters, food and drink from the shady forests and cool springs, and a happy social life with near neighbors, reinforced by associations in the rural churches.

Travelers through these rural communities a hundred years ago in the late summer and early autumn, saw abundant evidences of thrift and pride in the scaffolds of drying apples, peaches, and pumpkins; in the ash-hoppers and the seasoning cakes of home-made soap, and heard the merry music of the spinning wheel and the dull thud of the home-made loom. A short stay would have revealed to the traveler in those pioneer days other phases of this sturdy life in Egypt. Each head of the family was an expert in the making and repairing of his farming tools and implements as well as caring for many of the necessities and conveniences of the household.

The social life found healthy outlets in the quilting parties, the rag-tackings, the spelling bees, the log rollings, the house raisings, the shooting matches, and the square dances. Nor was the spiritual life neglected. The first public structure erected, after the homes were built, was the neighborhood church. There were no D. D.'s to be found among these God-fearing people, but there were many exemplary Christian characters in every locality.

Other agencies of culture were not lacking. Schools, newspapers, means of travel and communication, and the public forum soon made their appearance. It is true that the means of culture and the advantages of better living which are found in cities were lacking, since few if any of the population centers of Egypt had grown into towns of sufficient size to warrant the name city. In 1858 not more than a half dozen of the thirty-three county-seats in Egypt had reached two thousand population.

That these people lived in plenty and had some to spare, The Chicago Journal of 1872 can verify by this item:

"Fifty years ago, or in the summer of 1821," writes Charles Robertson of Arenzville (near Jacksonville), under date of February 8, 1872, to The Chicago Journal, "there was not a bushel of corn to be had in Central Illinois. My father settled in that year 23 miles west of Springfield. We had to live for a time on venison, blackberries, and milk, while the men were gone to Egypt to harvest and procure bread-stuffs. The land we improved was surveyed that sum-

---

NOTE—"The southern part of the state, known as Egypt, received this appellation as here indicated, because being older, better settled and cultivated, it 'gathered corn as the sand of the sea' and the immigrants of the central part of the state, after the manner of the children of Israel in their wants went 'thither to buy and bring from thence that they might live and not die!'" Quoted from "Davidson and Stuve's History of Illinois," page 351.

mer, and afterwards bought of the government by sending beeswax down the Illinois river to St. Louis in an Indian canoe. Dressed deer skins and tanned hides were then in use, and we made one piece of cloth out of nettles instead of flax. Cotton matured well for a decade, until the deep snow in 1830."

Many foolish explanations have been given as to why this region was given the name Egypt. One writer's explanation got into print and was widely read—"It is called Egypt because it has so many towns with Egyptian names;" similar it was to the school boy when asked "Why is the Mississippi river such a large stream?" said, "Because it has so much water in it."

The name Egypt was applied to portions of Southern Illinois long before there were any towns in the region, or even before the whites raised any Indian corn here.

The political situation in Egypt in 1858 was almost, if not altogether, lacking in interest. In the earlier years, from about 1818 to 1840, the people were deeply interested in public affairs; but the removal of the state capital from Vandalia to Springfield also removed the center of the state's political activities. The Republican doctrines, as they were known in the campaign of the year 1858, had found a scant few hundred supporters in the seventh, eighth, and ninth congressional districts. The Democratic party was seriously divided in Illinois. The two factions were known as Douglas Democrats and Buchanan Democrats. Douglas had grown in popularity in his party from 1854 to the time of his con-test, 1857-58, with Buchanan over the Lecompton Constitu-tion. Buchanan's followers in Illinois were those Democrats who favored the Lecompton Constitution or were federal officials in the state. There were at best only a few thousand.

In 1908, the fiftieth anniversary of the Lincoln-Douglas debate, intelligent citizens who remembered the political situation in Egypt in 1858, agreed that the Lincoln and Douglas debate at Jonesboro created little political interest in this end of the state. The Douglas cannon and a good brass band created a temporary enthusiasm which died down with their passing. Lincoln had only a few dozen shouters on the hot afternoon of September 15, 1858.

It was here in this Egypt, as imperfectly portrayed above, where Douglas said he would "bring Lincoln to his milk." The political interests at large took little stock in the joint discussion at Jonesboro. Only two or three of the metropolitan newspapers sent their representatives to the Jonesboro meeting, and these representatives confirm the opinion of local observers that political interest was lagging in Egypt in 1858.

LINCOLN'S FRIENDS IN EGYPT

Lincoln, considered geographically, was in no sense an Egyptian. But his ancestors in Kentucky and Virginia and the progenitors of the people of Southern Illinois in 1858, in Kentucky and Virginia, were of kindred stock.

There was much in common between Lincoln and the average Egyptian. Lincoln was among friends at the Jonesboro debate while Douglas was in the midst of strangers.

When Lincoln returned from the Black Hawk war in 1832, he ran for the legislature, but was defeated. He was a candidate again in 1834 and was elected. It was at Vandalia and at Springfield in the sessions of the general assembly that Lincoln began to make scores of warm friends in Egypt, and without reference to political party friendships.

Among the prominent public men in Egypt with whom he made friends were: John Dougherty of Jonesboro, Union county. He was a really great criminal lawyer as well as an influential politician. He was a member of the general assembly with Lincoln. Although a staunch Democrat, in 1858 Dougherty was allied with the Buchanan faction of the Democratic party. So bitter was he against Senator Douglas that, it is said, he promised Lincoln that he would try to get out a full state ticket for the Buchanan faction. Dougherty later bolted and allied himself with the Republican party. He supported Lincoln loyally during the war of the rebellion.

Dougherty attended the debate at Jonesboro as a silent listener. After the regular debate was over, there were loud calls for Colonel Dougherty. However, when he attempted to speak, he was drowned out by the howls of the Douglas faction and, in his stead, Usher Linder, a Douglas supporter, was called for and made a fine talk.

John A. McClernand of Shawneetown, Gallatin county, soldiered with Lincoln in the Black Hawk war and later sat with him in the legislature. They were opposed to each other in the national and the state campaigns in 1840. In fact, both were candidates for elector—Lincoln the Whig candidate, and McClernand the Democratic candidate. They met in friendly debate in Mt. Vernon and possibly elsewhere. President Lincoln appointed McClernand a Brigadier General at the opening of the Civil War and later raised him to the rank of Major General.

James Shields lived in his early manhood in Kaskaskia where he practiced law. He was a popular Irish Democrat. He held public office and sat on the supreme court. He served in the Mexican war as a Brigade Commander, and was commissioned a Brigadier General in the Civil War by President Lincoln. In 1842 Lincoln wrote some criticisms of the local administration and Mr. Shields took offense and challenged Lincoln to a duel. All arrangements were made and the duel was to be fought in Missouri, just over the river opposite Alton. The parties all repaired to the appointed spot, but friends intervened and the two antagonists returned to Alton apparently good friends.

Edwin B. Webb of Carmi, White county, was counted among the best friends that Lincoln had in Egypt. He came to know and to depend upon Lincoln from association with him in the legislature. They sat together several sessions as "Honest Whigs." Webb was a candidate for elector on the Whig ticket in 1840. He was a tireless worker in the ranks of that party. Webb's death in 1858 deprived Lincoln of a powerful worker in the dark days preceding the war.

Not the least loyal as a friend to Lincoln was Colonel John S. Hacker of Jonesboro, Union county. He served with Lincoln in the general assembly. It was through the esteem in which Colonel Hacker held Lincoln that the latter was able to count some votes from Egypt in the removal of the state capital from Vandalia to Springfield. He and his two sons, William and Henry, were politically all for Douglas in 1858, but personally the best of friends with Lincoln.

William H. Bissell of Belleville, St. Clair county, was the first Republican governor of Illinois. Colonel Bissell had won great honors at the battle of Buena Vista in the Mexican War, and had won praises in "an affair of honor" with Jefferson Davis. The common ground for Lincoln and Bissell was bitter opposition to the Kansas-Nebraska Act. In the 1856 Editorial Convention held at Decatur, Lincoln, who was present, was urged to take the nomination for the Republican party for governor at the coming Bloomington convention. Lincoln said he could not be elected, but that he could name a man who could hold all the old Whigs and draw heavily from the Anti-Nebraska Democrats. He had in mind Colonel William H. Bissell who was nominated at the Bloomington convention. It was in Bissell's behalf that Lincoln visited Belleville and spoke in Bissell's interests and aided in Bissell's election.

Lyman Trumbull of Belleville, St. Clair county, was a Connecticut Yankee. He came from the East by way of Georgia where he studied law. He sat in the twelfth general assembly with Lincoln. Here they began that friendship which was so real and yet so quiet. In the joint debates Senator Trumbull came in for a good deal of unfair criticism from Senator Douglas since he was not in a position where he could defend himself. Lincoln was elected to the nineteenth general assembly in November, 1854. He resigned before the legislature met, in the coming January, that he might be a candidate before the legislature for the United States senate to succeed Senator James Shields. The legislature was unable to choose between Lincoln and Trumbull for some time and Lincoln withdrew and allowed Trumbull to have the place. We may believe that Trumbull never forgot Lincoln's generosity.

Harvey T. Pace of Mt. Vernon, Jefferson county, sat

41

three sessions with Lincoln in the state legislature. They were both Kentucky-bred. Mr. Pace was not a politician, but a good business man. After 1848 the supreme court met regularly in Mt. Vernon, the seat of the Southern Supreme Court District. Lincoln killed two birds with one stone—he did business in the court and visited with Harvey T. Pace, his Kentucky friend.

Joseph Gillespie of Edwardsville, Madison county, went from the lead mines in northern Illinois to the Black Hawk war in 1832. There he met Lincoln, who he said was the strongest man and the best wrestler in the army. Lincoln was then only 23 years old. Mr. Gillespie became a lawyer. He sat in the twelfth general assembly with Lincoln. They were both active Whigs. Gillespie and Lincoln jumped out of the window of the church in Springfield in which the legislature was sitting in order to break a quorum and thus prevent the legislature from adjourning *sine die*. Mr. Gillespie is credited with setting in motion forces which helped greatly in the nomination and election of Lincoln to the Presidency in 1860.

On reading the address of the Honorable I. N. Arnold before the Royal Historical Society of London, June 16, 1881, on the life and character of Abraham Lincoln, Judge Gillespie said with much feeling:

"Sometimes I feel that my life has been a mere delusion; that I could have personally known and been on terms of intimacy with one who fills so large a measure of space in the world's estimation appears impossible and unreal."

Gustave Koerner of Belleville, St. Clair county, was a brilliant scholar and a great lawyer. He was elected to the thirteenth general assembly as a Democrat. He was also elected to a position on the supreme court in 1845. He was elected with Governor Joel A. Matteson, as lieutenant governor in 1852. It is thus seen that he was highly honored by the Democratic party. But in 1856 he was firmly allied with the newly formed Republican party. He was strongly anti-slavery in his belief. He became a hearty supporter of Lincoln and he introduced him to a great concourse of St. Clair county people in Belleville in the fall of 1856. He was a delegate to the Wigwam convention in Chicago where Lincoln was nominated by the Republicans for the Presidency. Mr. Koerner was on the staff of General Halleck in the Civil War and in 1862 was sent as our Minister to Spain. He wrote many books on law.

No man in Egypt stood higher in the estimation of Lincoln probably than Samuel D. Marshall of Shawneetown. He was a brilliant scholar, a profound lawyer, and a polished gentleman. He enjoyed a lucrative practice but gave of his time, energy, and of his means to further the cause of the Whig party. Marshall and Lincoln were in the legislature together and often closely related in the practice of law.

Another good friend of Lincoln in Shawneetown was Judge Henry Eddy, printer, editor, lawyer, volunteer in the war of 1812. Mr. Eddy established The Illinois Emigrant in 1818, the second newspaper established in the state, and was a very influential citizen in Southern Illinois. He was a Whig in politics, and tradition says that he and Lincoln were associated in several important law cases.

There were many other public men in Egypt who knew and admired Abraham Lincoln, some of whom were his political opponents, and many of them may have had more or less personal contact with the great commoner. Among these were: Zadoc Casey of Mt. Vernon; Dr. John Logan of Murphysboro; Samuel S. Marshall of McLeansboro; William L. D. Ewing of Shawneetown; David L. Baker of Kaskaskia; John Reynolds of Belleville; Sidney Breese of Carlyle; Andrew J. Kuykendall of Vienna; James M. Robinson of Carmi, and Alexander Jenkins of Murphysboro.

selves able to live where great men have trodden and not feel a sense of exhilaration, then, whether we be young or old, we have permitted something very precious to die out within us."

The author of these pages makes no claim that there are recorded here all the visits that Lincoln made to places in Southern Illinois, but he does believe that time and further research will reveal other occasions when Lincoln came to Egypt.

In his trips into Southern Illinois, Lincoln has been traced in the various places here named at the approximate dates given:

1. Lincoln Memorial Park, March, 1830.
2. Lawrenceville, March, 1830.
3. Belleville, April 11, 1840.
4. Alton, 1840-1858.
5. Waterloo, August 25, 1840.
6. Mt. Vernon, August 27, (?) 1840.
7. Carmi, August 29, (?) 1840.
8. Albion, September 1, (?) 1840.
9. Fairfield, September 2, (?) 1840.
10. Shawneetown, September 5, 1840.
11. Equality, September, 1840.
12. Morganfield, Ky., September, 1840.
13. Olney, June 2-3, 1842.
14. Gentryville, Ind., 1844.
15. Belleville, October 18, 1856.
16. Albion, September 19, 20 or 22, 1856.
17. Vandalia, September 23, 1856.
18. Thebes, 1854-1858.
19. Carlyle, March 18-19, 1858.
20. Edwardsville, May 17, 1858.
21. Edwardsville, September 11, 1858.
22. Highland, September 11, 1858.
23. Greenville, September 13, 1858.
24. Jonesboro, September 15, 1858.

25. Central City, September 16, 1858.
26. Alton, October 15, 1858.
27. Salem, June 9, 1849.
28. Salem, September 22, 1856.

LINCOLN MEMORIAL PARK, MARCH, 1830

Vincennes, Indiana, is a historic place, not only locally but nationally. The French settled Vincennes in 1702. The English held it from 1763 to 1779 when George Rogers Clark captured it in the name of the Continental Congress. Thomas Lincoln and his noted caravan crossed the Wabash river here in March, 1830. Within the last decade the states of Indiana and Illinois have jointly erected a bridge across the Wabash as nearly as could be determined at the exact route traveled by the ferry boat which carried the Lincolns from the Indiana side to the Illinois shore.

A state park of thirty-two acres has been laid off at the west end of the bridge where the Illinois Daughters of the American Revolution have erected a magnificent monument to memorialize the ground where Abraham Lincoln first set foot on Illinois soil. This monument is ten by twelve feet of sculptured limestone, portraying young Lincoln in bronze driving an ox team on this long trek. The title of the whole might be "Westward Ho."

While the state's commission laid off the trail of the Lincolns north from the ferry landing, it is now known that Abraham went by way of Lawrenceville, then north to Palestine.

The memorial erected by the Illinois Daughters of the American Revolution, the memorial bridge across the Wabash, and the magnificent structure marking the spot where George Rogers Clark received the final surrender from the British of the Northwest Territory make Vincennes a center of national history and a most interesting place on the Lincoln National Memorial Highway.

WHEN LINCOLN CAME TO EGYPT

A few years ago when state commissions undertook the task of marking out the route traveled by the Lincoln family in going from Gentryville, Indiana, to Decatur, Illinois, they found, by reason of a lapse of one hundred years, the task a difficult one. One problem was to determine where the Lincolns crossed the Wabash river—was it at Vincennes or at Russellville, ten miles above? There were supporters of both towns claiming the crossing place of the Lincoln caravan. The consequent uncertainty held in abeyance the building of a monument or expensive tablet to memorialize the place of the crossing.

The decision was finally made in favor of Vincennes, and a very appropriate memorial was erected by the Illinois Daughters of the American Revolution, at the western end of the bridge across the Wabash at Vincennes.

This road from Decatur, Illinois, to Gentryville, Indiana, by way of Vincennes, is officially known as the "Lincoln National Memorial Highway." Tourists from the territory to the north destined for the Smoky mountain region or Florida, are routed over the Memorial Highway, and others wishing to visit the Nancy Hanks Lincoln Park will, of course, take the highway which will be found exceedingly interesting.

Peter Smith of Petty's Postoffice, Lawrence county, Illinois, was a delegate to the Republican state convention at Springfield, May 9th, 1860. In a letter to his cousin, J. Warren Keifer, Esq., Springfield, Ohio, after discussing a few personal matters says:

"I attended our state convention on the 9th of May at which we nominated our state officers—there were about 600 delegates and I can truly say I never in my life saw congregated together so many noble intelligent men. But 'Honest Old Abe' was there, a head and shoulders above the rest, 'the noblest Roman of them all'—the observed of all observers, simple and unaffected in manners—sociable

48

and easy of access to the humblest of his fellow citizens. I had the honor of an introduction to Lincoln by my friend J. K. Dubois, auditor of state, who is from our county. Lincoln gave me a very cordial greeting and entered into conversation as an old friend and acquaintance. After conversing awhile I said to him, 'Lincoln, there is a rumor circulating in our region about you, and I want you to tell me all about it.' 'Well,' said he, 'what is it?' I said, 'Well, rumor says that about thirty years ago Abraham Lincoln was seen walking barefoot, driving an ox-team with an ox-wagon moving a family through our town of Lawrenceville. Is that true?'

" 'In part,' said Lincoln. 'About 30 years ago I did drive my father's ox-wagon and team moving my father's family through your town of Lawrenceville, and I was afoot but not barefoot. In my young days I frequently went barefooted, but on that occasion I had on a substantial pair of shoes. It was a cold day in March and I never went barefooted in cold weather.

" 'I will remember that trip through your county as long as I live. I crossed the Wabash at Vincennes and the river being high the road on the low prairie was covered with water a half mile at a stretch, and the water covered with ice. The only means by which I could keep the road was by observing the stakes on each side placed as guides when the water is over the road.

" 'When I came to the water, I put a favorite fice-dog I had along into the wagon and got in myself and whipped up my oxen and started in to the water to pick my way as well as I could. After breaking the ice and wading about one-fourth of a mile, my little dog jumped out of the wagon and the ice being thin, he broke through and was struggling for life. I could not bear to lose my dog, and I jumped out of the wagon and waded waist-deep in the ice and water, got hold of him and helped him out and saved him.'

"Lincoln is a man of the people. . . . We have good reason to believe that Egypt will be redeemed. Lincoln will

49

get a vastly increased vote over Fremont....Many other counties boast larger gains....in some counties in Egypt there were but two or three Republican votes in 1856, now they expect to carry the counties for Lincoln.....

"Yours truly,

"Peter Smith."

This letter is now in the keeping of the Lincoln National Life Foundation, Fort Wayne, Indiana.

When the final selection was made about the crossing of the Wabash, it was decided that the Lincoln caravan crossed at Vincennes and the route was laid out up the Wabash through the villages of Russellville, Heathesville, Palestine, Hutsonville and on toward Decatur.

Now Lincoln says he crossed at Vincennes and thence to Lawrenceville, eight miles west of the Wabash. The Mitchell map of 1837 shows a road along the river to Palestine; it also shows a road going due north from Lawrenceville to Palestine. The Mitchell map shows a swampy country between the Wabash and the road from Lawrenceville to Palestine. The route taken by Lincoln by way of Lawrenceville may have been to avoid the swampy lands along the Wabash.

Mrs. Ruth B. Burckhalter of Robinson says the tradition that Lincoln stayed over night at the old Dubois Tavern in Palestine is very persistent. It is generally known that Abe's father was poor and it does not seem likely that Abe would stay over night at a hotel when money was so scarce. However, it may not be so well known that Lincoln "the night before he left Gentryville, with the help of James Gentry, selected from the Gentry store about thirty dollars worth of notions—needles, pins, combs, knitting needles, knives, etc., which he peddled along the way to Illinois. This was a successful venture for after arriving in the Sangamon country, he wrote back to James Gentry that he had cleared

50

thirty dollars and had sold out all his stock." (From The
Missing Chapter in the life of Abraham Lincoln, by Mrs.
Ehrmann.)

BELLEVILLE, APRIL 11, 1840

The Whigs back in 1839 took time by the forelock and
nominated their state and national tickets nearly a year before the election. Their state convention was held early in
October, 1839, and the national, in December following. At
the state convention they nominated a State Central Committee of which Lincoln was chairman, a group of five candidates for electors: Cyrus Walker of Macomb; Buckner S.
Morris of Chicago, at large; Samuel D. Marshall of Shawneetown, first district; Edwin B. Webb of Carmi, second
district; Abraham Lincoln, third district. At the national
convention they chose William Henry Harrison for president and John Tyler for vice-president.

In Springfield in the winter following, when the legislature was in session, a new form of campaigning sprang up.
It was called the "Three day debate." This debate was informal and yet they observed a few simple rules. The Whig
cause was supported by Walker, Lincoln, Baker, Browning,
and Logan. The Democratic cause was upheld by Douglas,
Lamborn, Wiley, and Peck. The debate was so good natured,
informal, and helpful that a request was presented that the
debate be repeated and the request was complied with; not
only so but similar debates were held in nearby towns in the
spring of 1840. This form of campaigning brought Lincoln
and Douglas together in several smaller towns which gave
rise to the story that the great debates of 1858 were held in
these towns.

During the sittings of the legislature in Springfield from
December 9, 1839, to February 3, 1840, Lincoln was obliged
to remain in or near Springfield, but when the legislature
adjourned, he was "out on the hustings." His work was
chiefly in the central and north parts of the state, though in
April he ventured into Egypt.

51

WHEN LINCOLN CAME TO EGYPT

The new plan of campaign was to hold a county con-vention in each county in the state. At these county conven-tions a county ticket was put out and a great Whig rally was staged. It was planned that some one of the electoral or congressional candidates should be present. Lincoln attended as many of these county rallies as possible. Sangamon coun-ty held her convention-rally in Springfield in early April. It was a very large and enthusiastic gathering, Lincoln was present and was nominated for his fourth term in the legislature. From there he went to Carlinville where the Macoupin county convention and rally were in progress. Here Mr. Lincoln spoke. There was a monster parade of floats, bands, and people. Just in the midst of his speech, he was stopped by the arrival of a log-cabin float drawn by nine yoke of oxen.

Mr. Lincoln was on his way to Belleville and his road from Carlinville led him through the town of Alton, and the Alton Telegraph gives the following brief account of his stop in that place:

"A meeting of the people of Macoupin County, friend-ly to the Harrisburg nominations, took place at Carlinville on Monday, the 6th inst. The report of the proceedings has not yet reached us; but we have been informed by gentle-men present that it was the most numerous and enthusiastic ever held in that county. Macoupin has heretofore given the administration party large majorities. So numerous, however, are the changes which are daily taking place among her intelligent yeomanry, that strong hopes are entertained of the success of the Harrison Ticket at the approaching election. The meeting was addressed with great power and eloquence by A. LINCOLN, Esq. of Sangamon, one of the Presidential Electors and also by other gentlemen."—The Alton Weekly Telegraph, Saturday, April 11, 1840.

The meeting at Belleville on April 11th was the open-ing attack in Egypt of the Whigs upon "Little Van" and his policies. A battery of eight "big guns" was provided and the bombardment began early and continued till late at night. To provide variety, the log cabin, hard cider, coon-skin float was introduced. This was to become a marked feature of the Whig rallies for the 1840 campaign. Nearly all of the eight orators of the occasion were imported, main-ly from St. Louis, Mo.

The Belleville Advocate, on the 18th of April, 1840, gave liberally of its space to the report of the meeting. Though it gave two columns to the gathering, its descrip-tions were brief and its criticisms were not of very high order and were probably not the sentiments of the people of Belleville and St. Clair county. The introductory remarks were in part as follows:

"As we anticipated, a more perfect farce has rarely been exhibited in this or any other county, than the Whig Celebration on Saturday last. After an effort of three or four weeks, on the part of the secret committee of Belleville, this pantomime show came off. Notwithstanding the pres-ence of Whigs from Randolph, Monroe, Madison, and Sangamon counties, as well as the recent Whig mayor, de-feated Whig candidate for congress, and many Federal Tory lawyers and merchants from St. Louis, the *tout ensemble* of the Whigs did not amount to 300, rank and file.....

"We expected from the array of federal orators, that the people would have been informed something of the prin-ciples, of the measures that were to be carried out by General Harrison if elected; in this all were, like ourselves, disap-pointed.

"The first speaker denounced as traitors, all who would not support the federal candidate.

"Mr. Lincoln next followed, a federal candidate for elector. His speech was weak, puerile, and feeble. 'How dif-ferent,' remarked many of the Whigs, 'to what we had ex-pected.' Poor Lincoln! he should have rested his fame upon his printed speech, going the rounds in the federal papers, as purported to have been delivered by him at Springfield. He predicated his whole speech upon the sale of a one-eyed horse, for twenty-seven dollars, that happened to be sold by a constable during the day. To what slight accidents are we frequently indebted for our great things! How very fortunate for the Whigs, that Mr. Lincoln saw the sale of the one-eyed horse that day! He was thus enabled to prove that Mr. Van Buren caused it, together with all the other ills of life that us poor mortals 'are heir to.'

"The next speaker was a Mr. Primm, a federal lawyer from St. Louis.....His whole speech, however, consisted of vulgar abuse, empty declamations, and untrue assertions."

Other speakers were a Mr. Mallet, a Rev. Mr. Hogan, a Mr. Grimsley, a Mr. Dorsey, a Mr. J. L. D. Morrison of Kaskaskia, and a stupid Mr. Denny.

These all suffered at the hands of the Advocate's editor. The Advocate thought the Whig cause suffered as a result of this "great Whig Meeting in Belleville."

From the Belleville meeting, Mr. Lincoln hastened back to some apointments in the central part of the state.

The Whig campaign was probably better managed in the central and in the northern parts of the state than in Egypt, at least the Democratic majorities in the South were credited with carrying both the upper and the lower house of the legislature for that party. The Whigs had lost the state in the state election, but they still had hopes of carrying it in the November election. They now began to work with might and main.

WATERLOO, AUGUST, 1840

The Constitution of 1818 provided that state elections should be held in August, whereas national elections were held in November. Further, the election for governor in Illinois occurred half way through the presidential term. Therefore in Illinois only local offices were filled at the August elections in 1840. The state election contests aroused only local interest. The Whigs lost the house and the senate in the legislative elections. Their leaders were crestfallen, though not entirely discouraged. The national election was only three months off. After a few conferences, Alexander

WHEN LINCOLN CAME TO EGYPT

P. Field, Secretary of State, a former Democrat who had become an enthusiastic Whig, wrote to Henry Eddy of Shawneetown that ex-Governor Duncan, Abraham Lincoln, Ed Baker, and himself were going to make a thorough canvass of Egypt on behalf of the Whigs.

Probably of the four men Lincoln was the least known of all. He had friends in Egypt by the score, but the great body of people in Egypt did not know him. The strong man of the quartet was Alexander P. Field who had held the office of Secretary of State of Illinois since 1828. His home was in Jonesboro. He was therefore a full-fledged Egyptian, and had been a pro-slavery Democrat. Ex-Governor Duncan was an early comer to Egypt and had settled north of the "Big Hill" in Jackson county. He had a brilliant record in the war of 1812, and had been highly honored by the people of the state. Colonel Ed Baker was originally a resident of Belleville. He had served in the legislature. He was eventually to have a very checkered career. Lincoln's name was then in the making.

As Lincoln and Field were making their way to Waterloo in the fall drive, they passed through Alton and Belleville. They reached the latter city on Saturday, August 22, and arrived at Waterloo Sunday, the 23rd. They halted in Belleville and may have made short talks to hastily assembled groups in that city.

On Monday, August 24, 1840, notices were posted on the courthouse doors in Waterloo announcing that Lincoln would speak there on Tuesday, the 25th. Field and Lincoln both spoke on that day, and while details are lacking, it may be assumed that a goodly number of citizens was present. More especially are we justified in believing that many people heard Lincoln when we know that the Honorable Adam W. Snyder, a well known Democratic leader in Egypt, would speak from the same platform following the two Whigs. It was a common courtesy in those days—to invite your political opponent to speak from one's platform. It is thought that Joseph Lamborn may have assisted Mr. Snyder in the discussion. In that case the meeting took on the nature of a debate which was a common form of campaigning in those days.

The Belleville Advocate was a strong supporter of Van Buren and a bitter critic of the Whigs and it was quite active in the 1840 campaign. Lincoln and Field came through Belleville on Saturday, August 22, and spoke in Waterloo on the 25th. On the following Saturday the following story appeared in the Advocate:

"MISSIONARIES FIELD AND LINCOLN have again been sent forth on their circuit, by the 'Junto' of Springfield, to make a last effort in bringing their ignorant and heathenish Democrats of Illinois from out of their blinded and self-destructive errors.... One of these said traveling missionaries (Lincoln) held forth, we are informed, in Waterloo on Tuesday last (the 25th), to a large gathering of Democratic sinners.... But there happened to be present an advocate of the Democratic doctrines (Adam W. Snyder) who, when Missionary Lincoln had finished his incontrovertible sermon, got up and in a plain unvarnished discourse, left the poor missionary in an extremely pitiable predicament. These same missionaries, Lincoln and Field, were in Belleville last week (the 22nd), for the purpose of lecturing the besotted St. Clairmen."

From Waterloo, Mr. Lincoln journeyed to Mt. Vernon where we may assume he arrived by Thursday, August the 27th.

The author spent the larger part of a day in the historic city of Waterloo absorbing the spirit of a hundred years ago. He was kindly received by the Hon. Joe W. Rickert, now in his hundredth year, and his three daughters, Luella, Marie, and Marguerite. Mr. Lincoln's visit to Waterloo was in August, 1840, and Mr. Rickert was born the 9th of July preceding. Mr. Rickert was born in the historic city of Vicksburg, Mississippi, and he thought he had two good reasons why he did not hear Lincoln when he came to Waterloo in the Whig campaign in 1840. But Mr. Rickert was in a reminiscent mood and for the author it was a wonderful visit. A short call on Mr. Voris, editor of the Waterloo Republican, furnished several leads for further research. Waterloo is a city with a wealth of historic facts and of absorbing traditions.

MT. VERNON, AUGUST 27 (?), 1840

The Pace family of Mt. Vernon was one of the earlier families that settled in that region. Harvey T. Pace was a young man of twenty or more at the time of the arrival of the family from Kentucky. His eldest son, James M. Pace, was born in 1826 and a grandson, William T. Pace, was born December 22, 1853. These three representatives of the Pace family lived together in Mt. Vernon, Illinois, for more than a score of years.

The traditions of this family—grandfather, legislator, business man, and religious worker; father, teacher, lawyer, county superintendent of schools, mayor; grandson, lawyer, county judge, walking cyclopedia, hale and hearty, approaching his eighty-sixth birthday—make most dependable history.

Lincoln found occasion to come to Mt. Vernon oftener perhaps than to any other city in Southern Illinois. One of Lincoln's co-laborers in the 9th, 10th, and 11th sessions of the legislature was Harvey T. Pace of Mt. Vernon. And while these two men were of different political faiths, they were warm personal friends.

The sittings of the supreme court for the Southern supreme district were held in Mt. Vernon from 1848 to 1870, after which they were moved to Springfield. Lincoln's duties as an attorney brought him to this Egyptian city. On the occasions of his visits, he was always a welcome caller at the home of Harvey T. Pace, a wealthy, generous Kentuckian.

In 1840 Lincoln was a Whig candidate for Presidential elector. John A. McClernand of Shawneetown was a Democratic candidate for the same office. During the Tippecanoe canvass these two candidates met in a friendly debate in

57

Mt. Vernon. Harvey T. Pace and James M. Pace, then 14 years old, listened to this debate.

In 1923 the Joel Pace Chapter of the Daughters of the American Revolution, Mrs. Judge William T. Pace, Regent, erected a bronze tablet on the building now standing on the site of the old tavern or hotel. The new brick building is called the "Lincoln Building."

Judge William T. Pace says that he and his father went to the Jonesboro debate in the fall of 1858. He said there were no other people who went from Mt. Vernon as far as he knew. Asked if he remembered the appearance of the speakers, he said he did very well, and he recalled that the cannon nearly frightened him to death. When the Judge was reminded that he was only five years old at that time, he said, "Shucks, in 1856 I nearly yelled my head off hollering for Fremont, while all the other Paces were yelling for Buchanan."

A scrap of a legal document shows that Lincoln was *"guardian ad libitum"* for two hapless children whose descendants are still numbered by the score in Jefferson county.

1840
In memory of
ABRAHAM LINCOLN
Who on this spot
Delivered an Address
When he was
PRESIDENTIAL ELECTOR
Placed by the
JOEL PACE CHAPTER
Daughters of the
AMERICAN REVOLUTION
1923

WHEN LINCOLN CAME TO EGYPT

This tablet or marker is placed near the doorway of what is called the "Lincoln Building" on 10th street, Mt. Vernon, Illinois. The lower floor of this building is occupied by a large stock of furniture.

Perrin's history of Jefferson county, page 311, tells an odd story about this debate. Mr. McClernand spoke in the forenoon in a church in which court was generally held. He had a good hearing. Lincoln was to speak in the afternoon. When Lincoln and his audience arrived in the afternoon they found the room occupied. The sheriff and the judge, both of whom were Democrats, had decided that the church ought not to be used for political purposes and had opened a session of the court. Lincoln and his audience adjourned to the shady side of the Kirby Hotel, where Lincoln spoke from a goods box.

John A. Wall, a citizen of Jefferson county, when a boy lived in Mt. Vernon and worked at the Mt. Vernon Inn. It was in this hotel that lawyers who had cases in the supreme court and in other courts lived while in the city. Mr. Wall in a splendid history of Jefferson county put out in 1909, tells of the visits of Lincoln and other lawyers who came to do business in these courts.

He says that the lawyers were accustomed to sit around after the evening meal and argue politics. While the discussions were of a very friendly nature, yet the arguments were sometimes very earnest and often boisterous. When at a late hour the discussions were closed, Lincoln and other lawyers would hand over their boots to young Wall to be shined up for their appearance before the court the next day. From what one gathers, Lincoln was often a guest at the hotel which means that he had a goodly number of cases in the courts in the 50's, and in this way John Wall and Abraham Lincoln came to know each other very well. Mr. Wall says that with the money he earned blacking the boots of big men, he bought a pair of "red-top" boots and when he got them on, he felt as big as Lincoln or Douglas.

Mr. Wall says the lawyers did not always argue politics,

but some times they spent the evening telling stories. He said he remembered a story that Lincoln told one evening. Lincoln said, "When the State Capital was moved from Vandalia to Springfield, I followed it up trying to make a living in the law business. . . . I soon got a case that led me to attend court at Taylorville. I had no horse and so I told the old Rockaway stage coach to call for me the next morning. Meantime I greased my boots, put on my new jean pants, got out my old stove-pipe, and spruced up generally—looking as much like a lawyer as I could. When the stage came, it was full and I had to sit with the driver. After a few miles out the driver reached down in the box and drew out a raw twist of tobacco and after helping himself, offered it to me, saying 'take a chew, mister?' I thanked him, and said I did not chew. After saturating a mouthful of the stuff, he puffed it out against the wind, which caused it to come back over my hat, my pants, and my boots utterly destroying my previously handsome appearance, but he was not in the least disturbed. A little later he reached down and drew out a flask of 'red-eye' and after helping himself offered it to me. I again thanked him, and said, 'I do not drink.' He gave me a queer look and said, 'Mister, do you know what I think of you fellers who ain't got no small vices?' I said 'no.' Then with a leering look, he said, 'I think you make up in big ones what you lack in little ones; and I can tell by the cut of your jib that you are bad after the wimmen.' "

Mr. Wall came to admire Mr. Lincoln, and in 1861 when the call came for volunteers, he was one of the first to answer. Mr. Wall said he was proud he had blacked Lincoln's boots, and now he was just as proud to fight and serve at Lincoln's command.

CARMI, AUGUST 29 (?), 1840

Carmi was a very active political center in the 40's and 50's. It was the home of William Wilson, who was the chief justice of the state supreme court for a portion of these years. General John M. Robinson, United States senator, lived in Carmi. Edwin B. Webb, a member of the legislature, in these days lived in the young city, as did James Ratcliff, an early settler. It was on the direct road from Evansville, Indiana, to St. Louis, Missouri.

Miss Mary Jane Stewart and her relative, Mrs. J. W. Maffitt, live in the old log house that Miss Stewart's grand-father, General John M. Robinson, built in 1817. Much of the furniture is very old and some of it was taken from the old brick hotel still standing which Miss Stewart's great-grandfather, James Ratcliff, operated in 1840 when Lincoln was a guest there. This old log building was the first court-house used in 1819.

Mr. Webb lived across the street from General Robin-son in 1840. He was a great admirer of Lincoln. They sat in the legislature together and they were both "Honest Whigs." Lincoln was a candidate for elector on the Whig ticket in 1840. Mr. Webb secured Lincoln as the speaker for a "Tippecanoe" rally in Carmi probably in late August that year. The Whigs outdid themselves in enthusiasm. There was a regular log-cabin, hard cider, coon-skin parade, a big flag-pole raising, and a barbecue. The meeting was held north of the home of Senator Robinson in a park which is still there. It might be conjectured that Lincoln was in Mt. Vernon shortly before he came to Carmi. Much of the details of this visit have faded from view, but Miss Stewart and Mrs. Maffitt are certain that Lincoln had for interested auditors that afternoon Senator Robinson, Judge Wilson, Edwin Webb, and James Ratcliff.

The day following the rally, Mr. Webb drove Lincoln to Mt. Carmel. Mr. Webb had a daughter, Patty, who was to go to school in Mt. Carmel that fall and she accompanied her father and Lincoln and sat in the latter's lap all the way from Carmi to Mt. Carmel.

Miss Stewart and Mrs. Maffitt, when asked for the authenticity for the story, smilingly said they both were brought up in historical families, the facts as well as the traditions of history had been their meat and drink in all

61

these past years. The heirlooms from three or four leading families, their familiarity with early Illinois history, and their personal relationships in the past years confirm the validity of their traditions.

Mr. Chauncy Conger, attorney in Carmi, has made a careful study of Lincoln's legal activities in Southern Illinois, and he confirms the information that Miss Stewart and Mrs. Maffitt have given above.

ALBION, SEPTEMBER 1, 1840

Little Miss Patty Webb, daughter of Hon. Edwin B. Webb of Carmi, who later in life was known as Mrs. Frank Hay by her two relatives, Miss Stewart and Mrs. Maffitt, was accustomed to tell these two relatives of the long weari-some ride from Carmi to Mt. Carmel in the lap of Lincoln. Mr. Webb was generous enough to see that Lincoln got to his appointment at Albion the next Tuesday and he no doubt felt that Patty could forego the pleasure of the ride to accom-modate his best friend. Patty was booked to enter some sort of a school in Mt. Carmel, Tuesday, on the first of Septem-ber.

Lincoln and Webb were close friends. Both were mem-bers of the legislature, both Whigs, both candidates for presi-dential elector on the Whig ticket, and both heart and soul immersed in the Tippecanoe campaign. Webb was Lincoln's senior by seven years yet he was very deferential toward the Sangamon rail-splitter.

In working out a time schedule for this dash of Lincoln into Egypt, there are only a few dates that we can be certain of. We can start with Waterloo, August 25, assume Mt. Vernon, August 27, Carmi, 29, and en route to Mt. Carmel either Sunday or Monday. The big Albion rally was Tues-day, September 1st, and Shawneetown, Saturday, the 5th of September.

It may be asked why Albion was selected for the rally. It was the center of four surrounding counties and their county seats: Wabash and Mt. Carmel on the east; White and Carmi on the south; Wayne and Fairfield on the west; what is now Richland and Olney on the north; Edwards and Albion in the center. Twenty-five thousand people lived within a distance of 25 miles of Albion. A great highway extended from Princeton, Indiana, by way of Mt. Carmel, Albion, Fairfield, and on to Mt. Vernon. A similar road ran north from Carmi through Grayville to Albion and on to Olney. Then again Albion and Edwards county were Whig by big majorities.

But the Whigs were not going to have it all one way, for as was the custom in this particular campaign, both parties shared the platform. The champion of Little Van before the vast concourse was the Honorable Isaac Walker, a former citizen of Albion, then living in Danville. He was a candidate for elector in the northern congressional district. Tradition says it was an ideal day. The great numbers of visitors milled about the town and through the beautiful grove. The local people were organized into reception committees to go out on the roads and welcome the in-coming delegations, and at noon a great feast of barbecued meats was provided. The speaking was in a grove in the west part of the town.

Mr. Walter Colyer, the most prominent citizen in Albion in the latter part of the last century, was an editor and historian and has left brief day by day happenings of these years and also gathered up some happenings of the earlier days. It should be remembered that in 1840 Lincoln was only thirty-one years old and was practically unknown in Egypt, except by a few public men.

Mr. Colyer says, "In the autumn of the year of 1840 during the heated 'log cabin, hard cider, and coonskin' campaign of that year, the people of Edwards county were rallied to a great meeting at Albion where the Whig and Democratic candidates for presidential elector engaged in joint dispute. The disputants were Abraham Lincoln, then little known, and Isaac Walker, a former resident of the town.

63

WHEN LINCOLN CAME TO EGYPT

Lincoln appeared garbed in blue jeans and Walker in conventional black broadcloth."

Another writer has left this account: "Walker's polished and elegant appearance made Lincoln seem even more homespun and awkward than usual, but Lincoln won the crowd with his wit and an apt parody of the opening stanzas of 'Byron's Lara,' likening Walker to the 'self-exiled chieftain.'"

There was a sort of dramatic side to most of the Whig rallies in Egypt in 1840. People came into the towns on rally days early and it was necessary for the management to provide some form of entertainment for them. A monster parade was usually staged for about ten o'clock in the forenoon. Earlier in the morning organized groups, often young ladies, would be sent out the main highways to meet delegations coming from neighboring towns. Since there were not many bands in those days, organized choirs and mass singing from floats were quite common. All have read of the log cabin float. A real log house with an old 1812 veteran, the coon skins nailed to the cabin walls, the barrel of hard cider with a long handled gourd attached, with a hound dog or two made a display that attracted all and especially pleased the country people.

The traditional descriptions of the Albion rally in the early days of September, 1840, say it was the biggest rally in Egypt. The speaking took on the form of a debate which at that time was a new feature. Here there were other speakers, but the main participants were Lincoln and Walker.

FAIRFIELD, SEPTEMBER 2 (?), 1840

The Albion rally of the Whigs in the Harrison campaign was held, as near as can be determined, on Tuesday, September 1, 1840. Lincoln's next regular appointment was at Shawneetown, September 5. The Mitchell road map of Illinois, put out in 1837, shows a road from Albion southwesterly to Carmi and thence to Shawneetown and the dis-

THE PHILLIPS HOME, ANNA, ILLINOIS.

tance fifty miles. Another road only a few miles longer would take Lincoln to Shawneetown by way of Fairfield. In Fairfield he would find many Whig friends, one of whom was Daniel Turney, with whom he had served in the past four legislatures. Then he had another friend, William Virden, a real dirt farmer, a veteran of the war of 1812, a Whig, and an abolitionist, who lived on the road from Albion to Fairfield, at the county line. It may be remarked that the Whig plan of campaign provided that especial attention should be given at these rallies to the old 1812 soldiers. It may be safely predicted that Mr. Virden invited his friend, Lincoln, to go as far as the Virden home, remain over night with him, and reach Fairfield early Wednesday. At least the story of Mr. Virden's daughter would seem to indicate that arrangement.

Mr. Virden had settled in Wayne near the county line about 1825. He had built a large two story double log house with a "dog trot" 12 feet wide. There were two brick chimneys, the cracks between the logs nicely pointed with white mortar, and the shingles were rived, and shaved with drawer-knife, so his daughter said.

Mr. and Mrs. Virden had several children in this home. One, Elizabeth, was between six and seven years of age. Elizabeth married a Mr. Fancher and lived in her later life in Iowa where she died in 1915 at the age of eighty-two. She is said to have been a woman who spent her life in good works. She wrote a booklet of recollections in which she recorded this visit of Lincoln to the Virden home which was some eight miles west of Albion. One gathers the notion from Mrs. Fancher's story that her father invited Lincoln home with him just as farmers might do with any friend who was traveling.

Mrs. Fancher says she does not know what Lincoln was doing in that part of the country, but one infers that her father and Lincoln had been to a meeting and were late reaching the Virden home. She remembered that they sat

65

WHEN LINCOLN CAME TO EGYPT

up till midnight talking about the War of 1812, the Black
Hawk war, and kindred subjects.

Mrs. Fancher says that the next morning while the
family was at breakfast that it dawned on her that Lincoln
was a very large man, bigger than her oldest brother John
who was grown. After their guest was gone an older sister
remarked that Lincoln lacked a good deal of being handsome. The mother rebuked her and said "Handsome is that
handsome does."

On Wednesday Lincoln made his way to Fairfield, the
county seat of Wayne county. If this was Lincoln's first
visit to Fairfield it was not his last for T. P. Hanna, a
practicing attorney of Fairfield, says that the records of the
circuit court used to show that Lincoln had two civil suits
in the Wayne county court. In 1886 the courthouse burned
and the court records were all destroyed. Mr. Hanna says
his father, Robert Peel Hanna, who was a lawyer, was personally acquainted with Lincoln and had often told him of
the suits and the records. He claims that he has heard several
of the older lawyers discuss Lincoln's suits in the Wayne
county courts.

When Robert Peel Hanna came to Fairfield, he read
law in Judge Beecher's office. The Judge's younger brother,
also a lawyer, and young Hanna were very good friends.
Hanna was a Democrat, Beecher a Whig and later became
a Republican. In 1858 young Hanna and young Beecher
drove to Jonesboro, a hundred and ten miles, to hear the
Lincoln-Douglas debate.

In the days when Lincoln came to Fairfield, he found
the public men mostly Whigs and later Republicans. Among
these are mentioned Edwin Beecher, Charles Beecher, Bailey
Borah and his brother, William, father of U. S. Senator
Borah, Joseph T. Fleming, Jacob Hall, Joseph Barkley,
Charles Sibley, and William H. Robinson. The last two were
chairman and secretary, respectively of the Wayne county
Republican convention which endorsed Lincoln for the presi-

dency. Mr. Hanna was a loyal Democrat and was elected a member of the Constitutional Convention of 1870 from a Republican district.

The Prairie Pioneer, a newspaper published in Fairfield, published the following article in the issue of Thursday, March 15, 1860:

The following resolutions were passed at the Republican Convention, March 3, 1860:

Resolution No. 7. Resolved, That Honorable Abe Lincoln is the unanimous choice of the Republicans of Wayne county for the presidential nomination of the National Convention at Chicago.

Resolution No. 11. Resolved, That the proceedings of this meeting be signed by the President and Secretary and sent to the "Prairie Pioneer" at Fairfield, the "Chicago Press and Tribune," the "Egyptian Republic" at Centralia, and the "State Journal" with a request to publish the same.

(Signed)   C. Sibley, Chairman

Wm. H. Robinson, Secretary

Fairfield, March 3, 1860.

Some years ago a non-partisan Wayne county Lincoln Club was organized, having for its purpose the keeping alive of the spirit of Abraham Lincoln and the part Wayne county played in the movement which brought about his nomination for the presidency and later his election in 1860.

On the 6th of October, 1939, a beautiful commemorative marker was unveiled in the courthouse square which is intended to keep alive the spirit of Lincoln which prevailed in Old Wayne in 1860. The marker is six feet wide and five feet high of beautiful Georgia marble. Its broad front is largely covered by an aluminium plaque beautifully and appropriately impressed in bas relief, showing Lincoln in the upper center facing slightly to the left. To his right is the log cabin in which he was born, to his left in the distance is the White House, and below is Resolution No. 7.

67

WHEN LINCOLN CAME TO EGYPT

The dedicatory address at the marker was delivered by Governor George Aikin of Vermont. The people of Wayne county are justly proud of the part they played in 1860 in furthering the nomination and later the election of Lincoln to the presidency of the United States.

SHAWNEETOWN, SEPTEMBER 5, 1840

In 1840 Shawneetown was very active in the "Tippe-canoe Campaign." Samuel D. Marshall was the candidate of the Whig party for presidential elector in the first congressional district; Edwin B. Webb of Carmi was the choice of that party for elector in the second district; and Abraham Lincoln the candidate in the Springfield (third) district.

These three young statesmen had all sat in the House of Representatives in the 11th General Assembly from 1838 to 1840. They were a trio of kindred spirits. In addition to Lincoln's being a candidate for elector, he was the chairman of the Whig State Central Committee.

Lincoln and Field made a tour in 1840 of the southern part of Illinois in behalf of Whig national candidates. In this tour Lincoln spoke in Waterloo, Mt. Vernon, Carmi, Albion, and probably in Mt. Carmel, in Shawneetown, and in Equality. These speaking dates were in September and possibly as late as October. The speaking and the rally at Shawneetown were complimentary to Samuel D. Marshall, a fellow member of the legislature, and a fellow candidate, a fellow Whig.

Shawneetown in the first third of the 19th century was the most important town in Illinois. It was a commercial, social and religious center, as well as a political center.

The town located on the banks of the Ohio river was the crossing point of that stream for migration from Virginia and northern Kentucky toward the west. A ferry was established as early as 1802. It was also a "port of entry" for pioneers coming down the Ohio seeking homes in Illinois or desiring to reach Missouri. Morris Birkbeck's "Letters from

Illinois" shows an Emigrant's Trail from the mouth of the Chesapeake by way of Pittsburgh terminating at Shawneetown.

The commercial importance of Shawneetown was further enhanced from the fact that the greatest salt works west of the Alleghany mountains were at Equality only ten miles away. As early as 1813, a bank was established in the young town. A United States land office was opened in Shawneetown as early as 1812. The second newspaper in Illinois was established here in 1818, called "The Illinois Emigrant."

The Presbyterian church in the second decade was very active in missionary work in and about the new town. The young people of the more prosperous families were given college educations, usually in Yale. John Marshall's son, Samuel, spent four years in literature and arts and then four years in studying law at Yale. Sarah, his youngest daughter, was college-trained. She wrote "Early Engagements," and it is said that Mrs. Mary Todd Lincoln read the novel half through at the first sitting. This lady also wrote many poems and magazine articles. Four miles west of the county seat at Bowlesville lived George Eschol Sellers, Mark Twain's "Mulberry Sellers." He managed an extensive coal corporation, raised silk worms, and entertained distinguished visitors in a very fine library.

Public men, politicians, seemed to find sufficient excuse for making Shawneetown their homes. Among these may be mentioned:

Alexander Wilson, the first ferryman, tavern-keeper; sons and grandsons West Point graduates, and military leaders in the wars of 1812, Mexican war, and Civil war.

John Marshall, settled in 1804, merchant and banker, refused to make a loan to the city of Chicago for city improvement, security considered insufficient.

Henry Eddy, editor, lawyer, politician, and a friend of Lincoln.

WHEN LINCOLN CAME TO EGYPT

John McLean, state's first congressman, lawyer, United States senator, and a brilliant orator.

General John A. McClernand, lawyer, congressman, and a friend of Lincoln.

Samuel D. Marshall, lawyer, intimate business and political friend of Lincoln.

Miss Sarah Marshall, daughter of John Marshall, author and poet.

Samuel S. Marshall, lawyer, later resident of McLeansboro, belonged to the Marshall family, and a friend to Douglas.

Charles Carroll, merchant-prince, a warm friend to Lincoln.

General Michael Lawler, military genius, captain in Mexican war, and a major general in Civil war.

Ebon Ingersoll and his younger brother, Robert G. Ingersoll, both lawyers; removed to Peoria in the 50's.

J. M. Cunningham, in charge of the public land office in the 50's. His daughter, Mary, married John A. Logan.

Rebecca Daimwood, living near Shawneetown, inherited a tract of land from her uncle, Christopher Robinson. John Lane was the administrator of the Robinson estate and lived on the land, and Rebecca Daimwood, the heir, lived in the Lane home. She later married William M. Dorman. They made demand for possession of the farm. Lane applied to the court for authority to sell the land to pay a claim of about a thousand dollars against the Robinson estate.

William Dorman and his wife Rebecca retained as their attorneys Edward Jones, Samuel Marshall, and Abraham Lincoln, the fee being $1,200.00. To secure the payment of this fee, Dorman and wife executed a bond for a deed to the S.E. 1/4 Sec. 22, Town 9, Range 9 in Gallatin county. (Deed Record Book N, page 39, Gallatin county Circuit Court Records.)

Dorman and wife lost the suit in the Circuit Court. The case was appealed to the Supreme Court where Lincoln secured a decision in favor of the Dormans, January 15, 1852. (See Thomas' Lincoln Day by Day, pages 264 and 265.)

The lawyers not wishing to deprive the Dormans of their home and farm, agreed to accept a hundred dollars each in payment in full and to execute severally quit claim deeds, to Dorman and wife, to the pledged quarter section above mentioned. This is the explanation of a deed signed by Abraham Lincoln and Mary Todd Lincoln, a record of which is found in Record Book P, page 501, Gallatin county records. (Above records courtesy of Joseph L. Bartley, Attorney, Shawneetown.)

EQUALITY, 1840

To those who know the little village of Equality of today, it may seem strange that the two political parties of a hundred years ago should send some of their best political speakers to that town to hold a three-day debate on the issues of the campaign. But the Equality of to-day is not the Equality of 1840. A hundred years ago Equality was well known in all the territory from the Alleghanies to the Mississippi, and even in the border regions west of the Father of Waters.

The salt springs around Equality had furnished the source of that essential in good housekeeping for a great many years. Americans had controlled the manufacture of salt at Equality for more than half a century. Much capital had been invested in the industry and scores and even hundreds of laborers were finding remunerative employment in the various forms of labor necessary to keep the great industry going.

Men of means and business ability were identified with the salt works at Equality. The names of Willis Hargrave, Meredith Fisher, Jonathan Taylor, James Ratcliff, Timothy Guard, Broughton Temple, Joseph Castle, Andrew McAllan, Abner Flanders, George E. Sellers, John Marshall and many other public men prominent in Gallatin county were either

71

directly or indirectly interested in this prosperous industry.

Many of these and other public men of the community were interested in politics. It was therefore the most natural thing to do to arrange political speakings at Equality. There were hundreds of men connected with this industry in its various phases of labor. And it should be remembered that the Constitution of 1818 made it easy for residents to vote in the elections.

It was decided to give the voters of Equality a "three-day debate" on the doctrines of the Whigs and the Democrats and on the personal merits of Little Van and Tippe-canoe Harrison. The champion of the Democratic doctrine and of Little Van was John A. McClernand, a well known citizen of Gallatin county and a candidate for elector on the Democratic presidential ticket. He was to be assisted by Joseph Lamborn, a brilliant young lawyer, who was soon to become the state's attorney general. The Whigs were supported by Abraham Lincoln who was as yet comparatively unknown in the south end of Egypt. But he was to have the help of another brilliant young lawyer, Samuel D. Marshall, son of Shawneetown's financier, a recent graduate of Yale, and a candidate for elector on the Whig ticket. It will help to clear up party interests in Gallatin county to know that in 1824, in the slavery contest, Gallatin was the third most populous county in the state, being surpassed only by Madison and St. Clair.

As in other and later campaigns the "personal contact plan" was considered a good plan in Gallatin county. It was therefore thought wise by the Whigs to allow Lincoln to have the advantage of a "three-day debate" in Equality. While there were addresses made from the public forum, there was much time given to introductions, handshakings, story telling, and private interviews. Equality was a real labor center and little time and labor were lost in the formalities. We can readily see the advantage accruing from having such local help as McClernand and Marshall. There were friendly sittings, and campaign arguments were of the

72

most kindly nature. In fact, these four political leaders could say at the end of three days, "Well, we've had a jolly good time."

It is only ten miles from Shawneetown to Equality, and it is safe to presume that Whigs and Democrats living in the county seat frequented Equality while the "three-day debate" was in progress.

MORGANFIELD, KY., 1840

When, in the fall of 1840, it was known in Morganfield, Kentucky, that Lincoln would speak at Shawneetown in the Tippecanoe campaign, the Whigs under the leadership of George W. Riddell perfected plans to bring the young Illinoisan over into his native state. The young Whig missionary, like Paul who heard the cry, "Come over into Macedonia and help us," gave ear to his native people and agreed to lend a helping hand. Mr. Riddell was an enthusiast in many ways; and in Kentucky, the home of Henry Clay, it was easy to work up an enthusiastic Tippecanoe rally, and he not only kindled the flame in Morganfield, but came over to Shawneetown and soon had the Whigs in that young city not only willing to help but anxious to show Morganfield how to do it.

On the day following Lincoln's address in Shawneetown, or possibly later, his friends in that town accompanied him to the Kentucky county-seat. It was a good delegation —Lincoln, Henry Eddy, Samuel D. Marshall, twenty-six young ladies, one for each state, perched on a large canoe drawn by six white horses, a band of singers, a goodly number of Whigs in line, women, children, and a cannon.

When the cavalcade reached Morganfield, Kentucky, eleven miles from Shawneetown, Lincoln, his special friends from the Illinois town, the singers, and the young ladies representing the twenty-six states in the Union at that time, were all guests of Mr. Riddell at the town's best hotel. He found afterwards that his bill for their dinner was just thirty dollars.

WHEN LINCOLN CAME TO EGYPT

The speaking platform was not far from the hotel. The exercises were started off with music by the band, the canoe with the young ladies, the singers, and the voters in a monster parade. The procession wound up at the speakers' platform. With more music by the band and the singers, the audience was in an expectant mood. The cannon brought over from Shawneetown was loaded to suit the occasion. It was backed up against a large tree and at the proper time the torch was applied and there were thunderous roarings followed by thick clouds of smoke. When the people came to themselves, the cannon was lying on the ground in two pieces. The touch hole and about four inches of the butt end of the barrel were lying here, and a yard or more of the small end of the gun was lying there.

When the war came in 1861, Mr. Riddell cast his fortunes with the seceders. He was demonstrative in words and actions. At times he was very severe in his denunciations of the government and even of his neighbors. His case was referred to the semi-military authorities. He was arrested and confined in a military prison. The fare was not of the best and he soon tired of it. In fact, he would much prefer to be back in dreamy old Morganfield. With pen and ink he addressed himself to his old friend, Honest Abe:

> "After my compliments I would say that in 1840 I had you in tow at Morganfield, Kentucky. I put you and your friends up at the best hotel in town, and it cost me about thirty dollars. Now you have me in tow, and you are not treating me as well as I treated you. If you cannot do any better, send me home to my wife."

The story goes that Riddell was soon released and never tired of telling of his association with Lincoln, the young Whig orator from Illinois.

OLNEY, JUNE 2-3, 1842

Richland county was created by legislative enactment

74

WHEN LINCOLN CAME TO EGYPT

February 10, 1841. The county was sparsely settled and was not organized until a year later. The residence of Benjamin Bogard was designated as the temporary county seat. He lived near the site of the present city of Olney. In the afternoon of Thursday, June 2, 1842, five horsemen rode up to the county seat home of Benjamin Bogard. They were Judge William Wilson of White county and four lawyers— Levi Davis, Aaron Shaw, O. P. Ficklin, and Abraham Lincoln. These lawyers were "riding the circuit."

It was too late in the afternoon to hold a session of the court, so it was necessary to find lodging for the night in the homes of the pioneer settlers. This was an easy task and one that was common in those early days. On Friday morning the judge, the lawyers, the litigants, and interested neighbors all gathered at the seat of justice, the home of neighbor Bogard.

The judge took his seat, announcing that the circuit court of Richland county was now in session. Mr. Sawyer was appointed sheriff, a jury was empaneled, and the first case on the docket was called. The docket book was a blue paste-board back book with flimsy leaves. The case was Benjamin F. Park vs. George Mason, and the complaint, trespassing and cutting timber. The parties to the suit lived near the village of Parkersburg at the south edge of the county.

The judge very solemnly inquired if the parties to the suit were in court. Being assured they were, he asked if the parties were represented by counsel. Mr. Park responded that Mr. Lincoln and Mr. Shaw would represent the plaintiff; while Mr. Mason said that Mr. Ficklin and Mr. Davis would have the defense.

Lincoln opened the case. A large part of the day was taken up in the hearing of witnesses and in the argument of the learned counsel. The court rendered the decision in favor of the plaintiff. Mr. Mason was very much dissatisfied with the verdict and appealed the case to the supreme court

75

where it was heard and remanded. (See Scammon Book 3). This case lingered for a long time in the courts of Richland county.

The authority for this account of Lincoln's visit to Richland county was Robert K. Park, a grandson of Benjamin F. Park, the plaintiff in the above case. Dr. Park, 1817 Church St., Evanston, Illinois, is the great-grandson of the plaintiff in the above suit. The grandson referred to above says he has examined all the old dusty records in the circuit clerk's office in Olney for some other records of Lincoln but he searched in vain. His language is such that one is led to believe that the leaves in the court records showing that Lincoln had cases in the county seats have mysteriously disappeared.

Similar complaints have come to this writer and it may be there is some justification for the conclusion that once the records showed that Lincoln had quite a few cases in the lower courts in the early years. One regrettable fact is that within the past one hundred years, some of the courthouses having records of Lincoln have been destroyed by fire.

GENTRYVILLE, IND., 1844

In 1844 when Lincoln was a candidate for elector on the Whig ticket, Henry Clay of Kentucky, on the same ticket, was the nominee for the presidency. It was known that Lincoln was a great admirer of Clay. He therefore went into the campaign with great earnestness. The Whigs were the minority party in Illinois and were not so well organized as the major party. Lincoln's campaigning was therefore in a sense a personal matter.

Lincoln's method of travel was by stage or on horseback. In this campaign he traveled on horseback. It appears that his travels covered most of the state, but he reserved the eastern border counties of Egypt for the latter portion of the season for he doubtless wished to combine his work here with a visit to his old home in Gentryville, Indiana. Lincoln, by reason of economic necessity, introduced a new plan of campaign. It was of the nature of a house to house visitation. On entering a county Lincoln would invite some local candidate of the Democratic party to canvass the county with him. The invitations were frequently accepted.

These two friendly enemies often visited private homes, country stores, or find groups of people along the highway that would give them an audience. Their debates were brief, and the aim seemed to be personal contact. C. L. Kenner of Mt. Carmel, Illinois, wrote the author that his uncle, Alvin K. Kenner, sheriff of Edwards county at that time, traveled in this manner over that county with Lincoln. Tradition says that Lincoln was a visitor in the towns of Palestine, Robinson, Oblong, and maybe Lawrenceville in the fall of 1844.

In Ida Tarbell's History of Lincoln, W. L. D. Ewing is given credit for a good story. While canvassing with Lincoln, they were at a farmer's home late one afternoon. The farmer was quite an influential local politician, his wife also was politically-minded. Neither Lincoln nor Ewing had been able to get an expression of opinion from their hostess as to her attitude toward the two political parties. The wife announced that she would have to be excused as it was time to do the evening milking. Mr. Ewing saw his opportunity. He walked very sprightly by her side to the barnyard, and taking the milk-pail and the stool was soon merrily whistling away thinking how nicely he had put one over on his friend Lincoln. On looking around he observed Lincoln and his hostess leaning over the bars cheerfully discussing the political situation. When he had finished his task, Mr. Ewing handed his pail of milk over to his hostess who thanked him very kindly for giving her an opportunity to have so delightful a conversation with Lincoln.

Lincoln crossed the Wabash into Indiana on this trip and spoke at Bruceville, Vincennes, and Washington. At Bruceville the Democrats got up a rival meeting and as a result there was more noise than oratory. Lincoln now gave himself over to the task of reaching Gentryville, and to the delight of seeing some of his friends of former days. So far as we know no one went with him when he visited the last resting places of his mother and his sister. But it was a sad hour for him. When he returned to Springfield he wrote out his thoughts and feelings in ten verses, two of which, the second and the sixth, are as follows:

> O, Memory, Thou midway world,
>   'Twixt earth and paradise,
> Where things decayed and loved ones lost,
>   In dreamy shadows rise.

> Near twenty years have passed away,
>   Since here I bid farewell
> To woods and fields, and scenes of play,
>   And playmates loved so well.

Mrs. Erhmann in the "Missing Chapter in the life of Abraham Lincoln," page 93, says of the departure of the Lincolns from Gentryville for Illinois: "There were thirteen people in the historic trek. As Lincoln reached a point in the woods immediately west of his mother's grave, he left the wagon and ran up the slope to have a last look at Nancy Hanks' grave. He was loth to leave. His stay was so long as to cause his father, Thomas, to call out, 'Where has that boy gone?' Having been informed that he was at the grave, he straightway began to cry out: 'Hurry along, Abe, hurry up.' Presently Abraham came down the hill weeping."

While we may believe that Lincoln's visit to Gentryville and to Rockport was not essentially political, he responded to the request of old friends and made a few short addresses. The principal one was at the courthouse in Rockport in October, 1844. He is described as wearing a brown suit and a sort of riding cap. He was travelling on horseback.

BELLEVILLE, OCTOBER 18, 1856

The most notable gathering of the newly organized Republican party in Egypt in the campaign of 1856 was held in Belleville, October 18, of that year. Colonel William

WHEN LINCOLN CAME TO EGYPT

H. Bissell, the hero of Buena Vista, a beloved citizen of Egypt and of Belleville, then Egypt's largest city, had been honored by the nomination for governor by the Republican party at its state convention at Bloomington.

Because of a serious physical disability, Colonel Bissell had made only a limited canvass of the state. To make amends for any possible neglect of his own and surrounding counties, a great rally was planned for his home city and surrounding territory. The date was set for the 18th of October, only a few days before the election.

The gathering was well advertised and unusual efforts were made to provide the best campaigners. Bands, a monster parade, bonfires, and artillery were a part of the programme. The city was well filled by the noon hour and bands and the parade were busy shortly thereafter. Seats had been provided for the ladies and they were well filled with maidens, wives, and mothers.

The speaking began at the mid-afternoon hour and lasted till the sun was low. Thousands were present, hundreds coming over from St. Louis. There was singing and brief introductory speeches. More extended addresses were delivered by Lieut. Governor Gustave Koerner, a champion of Free Kansas. He was followed by Colonel William H. Bissell, destined to be Illinois' first Republican governor. Colonel Bissell was regarded as a polished orator. A Mr. Kayser spoke in German greatly to the delight of hundreds.

The orator for the afternoon, however, was Senator Lyman Trumbull, who had been bitterly attacked by Senator Douglas. He was formerly a Democrat but had been elected senator as an Anti-Nebraska man. His speech was mainly along national lines in defense of his action as opposed to the Kansas-Nebraska measure.

But the flood-tide of genuine enthusiasm came after the twilight hour, as the tired yet patient thousands expectantly waited for the coming of the great apostle of human freedom, Abraham Lincoln. Amid the illumination

79

of great bonfires, the singing and shouting of thousands, the music of bands, and the booming of cannon, Abraham Lincoln stood beside his friend Gustave Koerner who introduced him as his friend to the waiting throng. How simple and yet how grand! "Mr. Lincoln spoke with much feeling and great sincerity. He very earnestly praised the German stock for its love of liberty."

Lincoln could on this occasion speak with the assurance that he was loyally supported by three of Illinois' most able Anti-Nebraska defenders, Gustave Koerner, William H. Bissell, and Lyman Trumbull—all citizens of Belleville. The Belleville Advocate was not the least of the loyal supporters of Lincoln and the cause of freedom. It gave a whole page of the issue of the 22nd to the doings of the day—speeches, editorials, and local items. It said, "The palm, however, belongs to Mr. Lincoln; his was the speech of the day."

ABRAHAM LINCOLN
was a guest at
the John Scheel home
on this site and spoke
from its balcony
on October 18, 1856
This Tablet placed
BY BELLEVILLE CHAPTER
Daughters of the American Revolution
October 18, 1936.

This tablet or marker is placed on the wall of the Belleville Junior High School, west face, on Lincoln Street, Belleville, Illinois.

WHEN LINCOLN CAME TO EGYPT

Lincoln was entertained while in the city at the home of John Scheel. The home was at the corner of Lincoln and Illinois streets, a site now occupied by the Belleville Junior High School. B. Waldo Hilgard, a grandson of John Scheel, is a business man of the city. The Daughters of the American Revolution, Mrs. James W. Twitchell, Regent, have recently placed a memorial tablet on the Belleville Junior High School to commemorate Lincoln's visit and the site of the home where he was entertained.

ALBION, 1856

Albion, Edwards county, is very old and full of history. English emigrants settled here in 1818. There were really two distinct villages, the present Albion and two miles west the village of Wanboro. People usually say Albion, the home of George Flower, and Wanboro, the home of Morris Birkbeck. Two wrecks of old houses and the village cemetery are the only visible signs of Wanboro, a once flourishing town of three or possibly four hundred people. Corn fields and pasture land cover the site of the old "deserted village." Only the foundation stones remain to mark a once filled house of worshipers. Lovers of Egyptian history know well the story of "The English Prairie Settlement." Few are more tragic or dramatic.

These English settlers had been here less than a half dozen years when they were called on to help crush out a determined movement to make Illinois a slave state. Morris Birkbeck and George Flower were in the front of the battle line with James Lemen, John M. Peck, Benjamin Lundy, Hooper Warren, Edward Coles, Nathanial Pope, and hosts of others. Edwards county went 191 for slavery and 391 for freedom.

Edwards county supported the Whigs and later the Republican party. The older folks have said that the greatest outpouring of the people in the early days was on the occasion of the visits of Abraham Lincoln.

It was a rare opportunity the author had when he was

81

permitted to spend a large portion of an hour with Mrs. Anna Frankland, a woman in her 91st year, who remembers in much detail Lincoln's visit in 1856. She was then eight years old and even then she was an active participant in the stirring events of the day. She was one of a group of girls who were stationed upon a large float arranged by placing two farm wagons end to end and constructing thereon a long platform. This long float was drawn by six horses and its special mission was to go out on the road toward Grayville and meet and welcome the delegation from that vicinity.

Mrs. Frankland said the lady who had this particular group in charge decreed that all the little girls should wear dresses with short sleeves and low necks. The decree further provided that no one should carry a parasol. They rode happily out the Grayville road to the designated point where they should meet the in-coming delegation. Here they were obliged to wait in the sun till their arms and necks began to redden. When the visitors arrived, they all proceeded to the grove in the west part of Albion. The grove is still pointed out as the place where the rallies were held.

Mrs. Frankland remembers well how bewildered she was with the sights and sounds which greeted her when she reached the grove. She said there were men speaking on the platform, but that she does not remember that Lincoln was one of them. When the folks about her home and around the village spoke of her part in the day's doings, she said they called it the "Lincoln rally."

Mrs. Frankland has always been deeply interested in books, papers or conversations about Lincoln. She contends this day when she played even a small part in honoring the great man, has always been a bright spot in her childhood days.

The author called upon the best known man in Albion, the Hon. Nat Smith, ex-state Senator in the 52nd and the 53rd General Assemblies. He was three years old when Lincoln came to Albion and says he has no recollection of Mr. Lincoln's being there, but a certain happening which occurred at the Lincoln rally was one of his earliest recollections. "But Lincoln was here all right in 1856 and stayed at the 'Tavern!' " He was asked who kept the tavern and he replied that Mr. Bowman did. When Mr. Smith was asked if any member of that family was still living, he said Miss Kate Bowman, a daughter, lived just three houses off the square.

The author was kindly received by Miss Bowman. She has kept many articles of furniture from the old Birkbeck-Flower period. Her forebears were settlers in the English Prairie with Flower and Birkbeck. "I belong to one of the fast fading families of the first settlers," she said, when told that an effort was being made to collect information about the visits of Abraham Lincoln to various points in Egypt, and that it was said that her father kept the hotel where Lincoln tarried while in Albion: "My father, William Bowman, kept the tavern in Albion for many years," she continued. "It was a large two-story brick building, probably one of the first brick buildings erected in the village. It stood on the southside of the square just east of the present Masonic hall. When Lincoln came to Albion to speak he stayed at our house, the tavern. The old settee which you see on the front porch was then in the bar; there were other seats and possibly some chairs. The men guests sat in the bar and smoked, chewed, and talked politics. No, there were no intoxicating liquors sold in my father's tavern. Mr. Lincoln was sitting on the old settee and as I came close to him he took me in his hands and jumped me high in the air. He said he had a child about my size.

"I remember we all rode to the grove. I can remember very distinctly seeing a big wagon and some girls on it, there were some oxen hitched to the wagon. But the thing that seemed to impress me most was a woman dressed up to represent the 'Goddess of Liberty.' It was told her name was Miss Pope from Grayville."

Herndon wrote Trumbull on August 4, 1856, that "Lincoln has just gone southeast—down to Coles, Edgar, etc., and will go further south." Lincoln promised Jesse K. Dubois that he would speak in the southeast part of the state after September 15th. On September 18th, he passed through Vandalia. He spoke in a Fremont meeting in Vandalia on the afternoon of the 23rd. Here are five or six days in which period it is safe to conjecture that he spoke in Albion.

VANDALIA, SEPTEMBER 23, 1856

Lincoln was very much at home in Vandalia. He had attended two regular sessions of the legislature in Vandalia and part of another, from December 3, 1838, to March 4, 1839. At the latter date the capital took final leave of its home here on the Kaskaskia for its new home on the Sangamon.

Lincoln may have made occasional visits to Vandalia after the removal of the capital. We are very sure of his visit there in the fall of 1856 while campaigning in Egypt for the newly organized Republican party. He attended the Republican state convention at Bloomington, Thursday, May 29, 1856, and from that date forward, he gave much of his time to state and national politics. In the first national Republican convention, held in Philadelphia, June 19, 1856, Lincoln received 110 votes for vice-president. He was the nominee of that party for presidential elector in the Springfield district. He had virtually named his friend Bissell for governor in the state Republican convention. He was therefore obligated to give all his spare time to the support of that party.

Very little of his time was given to politics in Southern Illinois, but he was very busy in the central and northern part of the state. Jesse K. Dubois, whose home was in Lawrenceville, was a very good friend of Lincoln and though not a fluent public speaker, he was an excellent political worker. He wrote a letter to Lincoln inviting him to come into Egypt and help out in the campaign. Lincoln answered on August 19, and said that Trumbull would be in Egypt about the middle of September and that "I will strain every nerve to be with you and him. More than that I cannot promise now."

Mr. Dubois was impatient and thought another urgent call might bring his friend to this end of the state. He therefore dispatched the following note:

> "Lawrenceville, Illinois,
> "September 1, 1856.
>
> "Dear Lincoln:- If you could stop down here one day next week during our court and make us one big rousing speech, I would give you my hat, but if you can not I will think as much of you as ever.
>
> "Yours,
> "Jesse K. Dubois."

Lincoln was busy from the first of September to the 18th, in Atlanta, Jacksonville, Lincoln, Springfield, Bloomington, and Urbana. Mr. Angle's "Day by Day" story has this entry for Thursday, September 18th:

> "VANDALIA AND EN ROUTE. On his way to a speaking appointment, Lincoln learns that a Democratic meeting is in progress at Vandalia and stops over to listen. 'Long Jim' Davis, a personal friend, and a former Whig, singles Lincoln out for particular attack when he finds him in the audience. Chicago Democratic Press, September 27."

The speaking engagement which Mr. Angle mentions was, without doubt, the fulfillment of the promise that Lincoln made to Mr. Dubois on the 19th of August that he would be in Egypt after the middle of September. Mr. Angle makes no record of Lincoln's whereabouts on Friday, September 19, 20, 21, and 22nd. But on September 23rd, the Chicago Democratic Press locates him in Vandalia, and on the 24th, in Decatur. Since Lincoln was in southeastern

WHEN LINCOLN CAME TO EGYPT

Egypt but once in the fall of 1856, and since September 21st was Sunday, the great Republican rally in Albion which Mrs. Anna Frankland, Miss Kate Bowman, and ex-Senator Smith remember so vividly must have been held on Friday, the 19th, Saturday, the 20th, or Monday, the 22nd. It seems then that Lincoln was in Egypt only on three occasions—Albion, Vandalia, and Belleville—for the Bissell-Fremont campaign.

THEBES, 1854-1858

The county seat of Alexander county was located at Thebes on the Mississippi river twenty-five miles above Cairo from 1845 to 1860. The old stone building whose walls are two feet thick sits high on the side of the bluff as it did a hundred years ago. It now houses the Community Library. It is two stories high with an overhanging pediment supported by Greek pillars. The building was constructed from native stone taken from the bluff just back of the structure. In the first story are two dungeons with only two small openings in each for ventilation. The dungeons have massive oak doors.

From the second story one may look down on the Mississippi far below and upon the Missouri shore line a mile or more away. It is a beautiful view and its traditions fill the imagination with the life of a hundred years ago.

H. P. Marchildon, a merchant of Thebes, says his fore-bears were residents of Thebes from a very early day. He tells of a boy by the name of Smith who worked in the hotel in the days when Thebes was the county seat. The boy had one task that he seemed to remember very well. It was to shine up the boots of the guests at night so that the lawyers might appear well groomed in court the next day. Mr. Smith as an old man lived in East Prairie, Missouri, and always inquired of traveling men about Thebes and told of his acquaintance with Lincoln when he practiced law in the old courthouse.

As related elsewhere, one of Lincoln's best friends in

86

Egypt was John S. Hacker of Jonesboro and Cairo. Colonel Hacker had two sons and two daughters. The latter were educated in New Orleans and in St. Louis. The sons were educated in the East—William at West Point, Henry in a medical school in Philadelphia. William was a lawyer at nineteen, a contender with Colonel John Dougherty, Egypt's most noted lawyer. He held office in Washington by favor of Senator Douglas and was married in that city. A son was born in Annapolis, Md., in 1852 and shortly thereafter the family moved to Cairo. Here the father pursued his profession of law.

The son, J. L. Hacker, did not take kindly to either law or politics, but took to the water like a fish. He was a clerk, a pilot, and later a captain—in all 68 years out of 88 years of his life. A letter from Captain Hacker of recent date says that it has always been his understanding that his father and Lincoln rode the Cairo circuit together and, of course, attended court together in Thebes.

EDWARDSVILLE, MAY 17, 1858

The student of the national political campaign of 1858 knows that there was a division in the Democratic party in that campaign. One faction was known as the Douglasites, the other the Buchananites. He will also recall that the Republican leaders were working to prevent this break from healing. In volume IV, page 166, of the Centennial History of Illinois, it says: "Separate Democratic tickets would mean easy Republican victory; the hopes of the Lincolnites fed upon the bitterness toward Douglas of prominent Buchanan men. Dr. Charles Leib of Chicago and even Colonel John Dougherty of Jonesboro lent aid and comfort in this direction by their assurances to both Senator Trumbull and Lincoln that the national democracy (the Buchanan party in Illinois) would without fail remain in the field with separate candidates in every county and congressional district."

To prevent the Buchananites from going over to the

87

Douglas faction, certain Republicans pretended to favor Douglas hoping to drive the Danites from the "Little Giant." One such radical Republican was M. W. Delahay of Alton, a very good friend to Lincoln. Mr. Delahay made Douglas speeches apparently with the consent of Lincoln. It seemed to be agreed that he should do this till all the counties and congressional districts had put out their Buchanan, or national Democratic tickets, then he would return to the Republican fold.

On May 18, 1858, Delahay and Lincoln went from Alton to Edwardsville where Lincoln made a rousing Republican speech. It is presumed that Delahay spoke for Douglas on that occasion. "He remained in the field until the Buchanan convention nominated its state ticket; then according to arrangement, he came out for Lincoln." Mr. Delahay moved to Kansas and was responsible for Lincoln's visit to that state on a short speaking tour in December, 1859.

EDWARDSVILLE, SEPTEMBER 11, 1858

Mr. Lincoln spent Sunday, September 5th, in Springfield. On Monday he made his way to Monticello, Piatt county. Thence to Mattoon in the forenoon of Tuesday and was at Paris, Edgar county, in the afternoon, accompanied by Horace White. At Paris they met Owen Lovejoy, a powerful anti-slavery campaigner, who spoke at night.

Lincoln was now headed for Edwardsville and Greenville, his last appointments before Jonesboro. He passed through Hillsboro where he spoke, and reached Edwardsville in the afternoon of Friday. Here he was received by one of his most loyal friends, Judge Joseph Gillespie. He remained the Judge's guest till Sunday morning. The speech of Lincoln in the afternoon of Saturday was one of the most powerful appeals he made in the campaign. Mr. White thinks that there was an emotional air surrounding the occasion which he did not observe at any other gathering.

Edwardsville was the home of Judge Joseph Gillespie,

one of Lincoln's best friends. He and Lincoln were born the same year, they were both self-educated, both served in the Black Hawk war, both were "Honest Whigs." They served one term in the legislature together, the 12th General Assembly. Judge Gillespie served in the state senate from 1847 to 1859. He was therefore in close touch with Lincoln in Springfield for several years. In 1856 he was a candidate for elector on the Fillmore ticket, but by 1858 he was heart and soul with Lincoln.

Lincoln came to Edwardsville, on his way to Jonesboro, Saturday, September 11, 1858. He spoke that day to an enthusiastic gathering of Republicans in Edwardsville, and Judge Gillespie presided.

Horace White in "Herndon's Life of Lincoln," page 114, Vol. II., says: "At Edwardsville I was greatly impressed with Mr. Lincoln's speech....I took down passages which as I read them now, after the lapse of thirty-one years, bring back the whole scene with vividness before me—the quiet autumn day in the quaint old town; the serious people clustered around the platform; Judge Joseph Gillespie acting as chairman; and the tall, gaunt, earnest man....appealing to his old Whig friends, and seeking to lift them up to his own level."

It was here in Edwardsville that Lincoln answered the question put by an inquirer: "What is the difference between the Democrats and the Republicans?" Mr. Lincoln replied: "The difference between the Republican and the Democratic parties on the leading issues of this contest, as I understand it, is that the former consider slavery a moral, social, and political wrong, while the latter do not consider it either a moral, a social, or a political wrong....I will not affirm that the Democratic party consider slavery morally, socially, and politically right, though their tendency to that view has, in my opinion, been constant and unmistakable for the past five years. I prefer to take as the accepted maxim of the party, the idea put forth by Judge Douglas, that he don't care whether slavery is voted down or voted up....Every measure of the Democratic party of late years, bearing directly or indirectly on the slavery question, has corresponded with this notion of utter indifference, whether slavery or freedom shall outrun in the race of empire across to the Pacific. Every measure, I say, up to the Dred Scott decision, where it seems to me, the idea is boldly suggested that slavery is better than freedom."

It was at the afternoon meeting that a large committee presented Lincoln with an earnest request that he come to Highland that night and address the people of that village. Lincoln was fully aware of the German thought and senti-ment there toward the anti-slavery cause. It was rapidly moving in the right direction, and he could not afford to miss this opportunity to strengthen them in the faith. He promised to meet them at "early candle light."

On Sunday, September the 12th, Judge Gillespie and Lincoln drove from Edwardsville to Greenville by way of the town of Highland. The distance is forty miles. Great preparations had been made in Greenville for this rally. Douglas had spoken there a short time before and the Re-publicans were anxious to have as large an attendance as the Democrats had. Lincoln and Judge Gillespie both spoke to the assembled thousands on Monday, September 13, 1858.

HIGHLAND, SEPTEMBER, 1858

Highland, Madison county, was settled by Germans and Swiss in 1836. It is situated in the northern part of the famous Looking Glass Prairie, one of the most noted prairie areas in all the state. Charles Dickens had a great desire when in St. Louis in 1842, to see Looking Glass Prairie. Friends accompanied him to its western edge near Lebanon where his desire was abundantly gratified. Not only in England had this wonderful expanse of country often been described, but the first German immigrants had sent back descriptions of this wonderful country. The German population in St. Clair and Madison counties had grown by leaps and bounds from 1830 to 1858.

WHEN LINCOLN CAME TO EGYPT

These German people were freedom-loving. As early as 1824 when the slavery interests attempted to make Illinois a slave state, the counties of St. Clair and Madison helped greatly to save the day.

Gustave Koerner, a university trained immigrant, who settled in Belleville, was the undisputed leader of the political thought of these German citizens. He was greatly honored by the Democratic party until 1856, when there appeared to be a plan in that party to extend slavery into the great Northwest. Mr. Koerner, who at that time was the lieutenant governor of the state, deserted the Democrats and joined his fortunes with the Anti-Nebraska or Republican party. Very naturally the body of German citizens in Southern Illinois followed him whom they had always trusted.

It is easy to understand why the Germans of Highland, when they knew Lincoln, the great apostle of freedom, was to speak in Edwardsville on Saturday, September 11th, and that he was due in Greenville on Monday, the 13th, and in Jonesboro on Wednesday, the 15th, hit upon the plan of inviting him to come to their town and talk to them upon the issues of the day following his speech at Edwardsville. Although the day had made heavy demands upon his physical resources, Lincoln agreed to comply with their request.

After speaking Saturday evening in Highland, Lincoln returned to Edwardsville where he remained over night with Judge Gillespie. On Sunday, September 12th, Judge Gillespie and Lincoln drove to Greenville by way of Highland, a distance of nearly forty miles. In the diary of Wm. S. Wait, a very prominent citizen of Greenville, is an entry—"Monday, September 13, 1858, Abe Lincoln speaks in Greenville today, and J. Gillespie."

The Greenville Advocate of date of February 12, 1934, in speaking of the events of the visit of Lincoln in 1858 says: "It was thought for some time that Lincoln, like Douglas, had driven to Greenville from Carlyle. But Lincoln letters to Judge Gillespie preserved by the latter's son,

91

WHEN LINCOLN CAME TO EGYPT

Charles T. Gillespie, make it plain that Mr. Lincoln and Judge Gillespie drove from Edwardsville through Highland for his speech here in September, 1858."

Carlyle, the county seat of Clinton county, is situated on the Kaskaskia river fifty miles east of St. Louis. It is on the old wagon road from St. Louis to Vincennes. It is a very old town and is on the conservative order. The old and the new are today side by side, for a wonderful concrete bridge now spans the raging Kaw, whereas only a stone's throw away still swings the old suspension bridge which did duty from 1860 to the end of the last century.

In 1857, Robert Truesdail from Girard, Pennsylvania, established the Truesdail Hotel on the northeast corner of the square. Mr. Truesdail was a good hotel man for he never had any opposition in the hotel business. This hotel has remained in the hands of this family for about eighty years. The register Mr. Truesdail used in 1858 was a plain blank page book.

Several decades ago a gentleman chanced to see the old register and asked permission to box it up for preservation. It was boxed with a glass top so all may see. It sits on the hotel counter. The story as first told was that Lincoln's name was among the notables. But it is not there. And this is the explanation now offered: On the dates shown (No one knows which date), a "bunch of newspaper men" came into town. When they alighted from the stage coach, some friends of Lincoln "kidnapped" him, put him on a farmer's hay-wagon and drove him to the home of a Doctor Moore where a bountiful dinner was served to the "kidnappers" and the noted guest. The other men, supposed to be newspaper men, went to the hotel and registered as appears on the page to this day. They took their departure. The daughter of the hotel keeper, Miss Lydia Truesdail, at that time about sixteen years old, was attending Greenville College and that afternoon she saw these newspaper men pass through Greenville on their way to Vandalia and Abraham Lincoln was with them.

1858   March   18

TRUESDAIL HOTEL

Will Henry	Cincinnati St Louis
M C McLaughlin	Cincinnati St Louis
C Carpenter	Pappa Mich
W Firth	illegible
S A Douglas	Senator from Illinois
Lyman Trumbull	Washington D C
March 19 1858	
Michel Nickerson	St Louis
John McCheeke	Bond co Ill
M Bennett & family	illegible
O B Clam	Olney
John Adams	Rock Island
A C Roberts	Rockford Ill
A B Parter	Mt Pleasant Iowa
Lewis Bailey	Frankfort
Wm Holland	illegible
Robert Ridley	"One of the boys"
John Smith Esq	Keokuk Iowa
Horace Greeley	New York Tribune
Gordon Bennett	of the Herald

This is an exact copy of a page of the Truesdail Hotel register at Carlyle, Illinois, said to have been written on the dates indicated above. The senators' names are apparently written by the same person and in the same ink. The date at the top of the page, "1858   March   18," apparently is not in the same hand writing nor in the same ink as the body of the page. Neither is the date in the middle of the page, "March   19   1858."

Mr. Fisk, the present clerk, is the son of Mrs. Lydia Truesdail Fisk, who in her later life, her son says, made a

93

very searching effort to get at the truth of the "kidnapping," the hayride, and the dinner, and Mr. Fisk says she often told him that the report was true.

The troublesome thing about all this is that in March up to the twenty-third of the year 1858, the bill to admit Kansas under the Lecompton Constitution was before the United States senate and Senator Douglas was bitterly opposed to the passage of the bill. Not only so but Senator Douglas was sick in bed most of that time and the final action on the bill was deferred until he was able to come into the senate and deliver his final objection, which he did at a night session on the 22nd of March, 1858, only four days after he was a guest at the Truesdail Hotel in Carlyle. It should be said that Senator Trumbull was standing loyally by Senator Douglas in Washington in those trying days.

In a recent letter from C. E. Truesdail of the hotel, the grandson of the original proprietor, he states that the home to which Lincoln was taken when he was "kidnapped" was that of A. C. Gray, a lawyer of Carlyle.

Again the court records of Logan county reveal that Lincoln had a case in the court at Lincoln, the county seat, on Thursday, March 18, 1858. The tradition does not show whether Lincoln was in Carlyle on the 18th or the 19th.

This page of the Truesdail Hotel register has been "boxed in" for a goodly number of years and sitting on the hotel counter where all may see. It has been seen and studied by many people, and it is not known that any one has ever questioned the authenticity of the signatures. The fact that Douglas and Trumbull registered on the eighteenth and Greeley and Bennett did not register until the nineteenth does not seem to have disturbed any one. Nor does the question as to which group—the politicians, Douglas and Trumbull, or the newspaper men, Greeley and Bennett—Lincoln was traveling with.

The present proprietors of the Truesdail Hotel are

grandchildren of Robert Truesdail, who eighty-two years ago founded the hotel. It should be said that they are mighty fine people, and keep a very fine establishment. They lean to the theory that the signatures are genuine, and believe that the five noted men were in Carlyle as shown by the register and borne out by tradition.

The above story is related for the reason that it is currently believed that Lincoln and Douglas were at this hotel in Southern Illinois, but the author is rather of the opinion that it has no foundation in fact.

GREENVILLE, SEPTEMBER 13, 1858

The facts and traditions relative to the visit of Lincoln to Greenville, Bond county, September 13, 1858, have been well preserved. The Greenville Advocate was founded by Jediah F. Alexander, February 11th, 1858, as a champion of the cause of Abraham Lincoln. On the seventy-fifth anniversary of the visit of Lincoln to Greenville, February 12, 1934, the Advocate published an anniversary edition of seven sections, 72 pages, one section devoted to a restatement of the facts and the traditions of the events of that noted occasion.

On Sunday, September 12, 1858, Judge Joseph Gillespie drove with Lincoln through the village of Highland—a settlement of thrifty Germans who had settled there in 1836—on their way to Greenville where Lincoln was to speak the next day. Douglas had filled an appointment in Greenville early in August. He had addressed a large gathering and the Republicans were hoping they could equal or surpass the Democratic crowd.

On arriving at Greenville, Lincoln and Gillespie put up at the Franklin House, a good hostelry run by Thomas S. Smith. Although it was Sunday, at night the homes were all lighted up with long rows of candles. The speaking on Monday was held in the Colcord grove in the west part of the town where Douglas had spoken. There were people present from every part of the county and some from the adjoining counties.

Dr. Samuel Colcord of New York City, a former citizen of Greenville, said about the time of the anniversary, that he was at the rally in 1858 and remembered many features of that occasion. He quoted Lincoln's opening paragraph which, he said, was too mild for a vigorous debater. Lincoln said:

"I understand my friend, Judge Douglas, was here the other day (August 4, 1858). He is a great jurist, an eminent lawyer, a fine debater, and an able statesman, who has done honor to his state and country."

Will C. Carson, editor of the Advocate, and a nephew of Dr. Colcord, interviewed his uncle in 1930, relative to the visits of Lincoln and Douglas in 1858. The Doctor was then in his eighty-first year, but he recalled very distinctly the subject of the discussion and also many incidents of the visits of Douglas and Lincoln. He remembered that the day that Douglas spoke, the town and the grove where Douglas spoke were literally covered with large posters advertising that Lincoln would speak in town in a few days. He said his father was an eastern man, a radical abolitionist, and a great friend of Lincoln. The Doctor thought Lincoln was very mild in his charges and criticisms of Douglas, but believed that made friends for Lincoln.

The Daughters of the American Revolution, through Mrs. Charles Davidson, Vice President of the Middlewest Division of the National Society, have erected a bronze tablet to mark and preserve the place where Lincoln spoke. Mrs. Davidson says that her father and mother, Mr. and Mrs. Abraham McNeil, both attended the speaking in 1858 and that they were accustomed to repeat many of the features of that interesting day.

One thing the older people told the youngsters about was the wonderful illumination of the entire town on Sun-

WHEN LINCOLN CAME TO EGYPT

The following letter will explain why Mr. Lincoln could not at that time accommodate his editor friend:

"Summer 1858.

"Mr. J. F. Alexander,
"Greenville, Illinois.
"My Dear Sir:- I should be with Judge Douglas at your town on the 4th, had he not intimated in his published letter, that my presence would be considered an intrusion. I shall soon publish a string of my appointments, following his present track, which will bring me to Greenville about the 11th of September. I hope to have Judge Trumbull with me.

"Yours truly,

"A. Lincoln."

Lincoln was in Edwardsville on the eleventh and did not reach Greenville till the thirteenth, and instead of Judge Trumbull for a companion, he had Judge Joseph Gillespie.

THIS TABLET DEDICATED TO
The Memory Of
ABRAHAM LINCOLN
Who Spoke Here September 13, 1858
Erected By
DAUGHTERS OF THE AMERICAN REVOLUTION
September 13, 1935

This tablet or marker was erected by the "Benjamin Mills" chapter and is attached to a large boulder in the yard of John Buscher on a prominent street in Greenville where all may see it who pass that way.

WHEN LINCOLN CAME TO EGYPT

Sunday, September 12th, Judge Gillespie accompanied Lincoln to Greenville where he had an appointment to speak on Monday, the 13th. This date is fixed by the files of the Greenville Advocate. Letters from Lincoln to Judge Gillespie, now in the keeping of the descendants of the Gillespie family, determine that Lincoln remained over night in Edwardsville, and that the Judge and Lincoln drove through the country to Greenville by way of the German community of Highland.

Dr. Samuel Colcord of New York City, a former citizen of Greenville, said in 1930, that as a boy of nine years, he listened very attentively to Lincoln's speech in Greenville and that Lincoln came to him after the speaking was over and shook hands, patted him and told him he was a good listener. Dr. Colcord stated that as Lincoln and Judge Gillespie approached Highland, the Judge said to Lincoln, "These people are Germans, but mighty fine people and good citizens. They might ask you to take a drink with them. I am giving you warning in time." Mr. Lincoln was quiet for a while and said, "I will not do so."

ALTON, 1840 TO 1858

Alton became a political and a commercial center early in the first half of the last century. The first state penitentiary was located in Alton in 1833. Lovejoy, the abolitionist editor, was murdered there in 1837. The Illinois troops bound for the Mexican war were embarked there for New Orleans in 1846. The last of the joint debates between Lincoln and Douglas was held in Alton on October 15, 1858.

Lincoln was a frequent visitor in Alton though some of his visits there were merely as a passer-by on his way to other points.

The Alton Weekly Telegraph of Saturday, April 11, 1840, has this item: "A. Lincoln, Esq. of Sangamon county, one of the Presidential Electors, addressed the citizens of Alton on last Thursday evening, April 9, at the old Court

99

room, on the great questions at issue between the people and the office-holders. Although not more than two or three hours previous notice could be given of the intended meeting, the room, which is very spacious, was crowded to excess, and his speech which, although highly argumentative and logical, was enlivened by numerous anecdotes, was received with unbounded applause and left a very favorable impression on the minds of his auditors."

On August 21, 1840, Lincoln passed through Alton on his way to Waterloo. He was accompanied by Alexander P. Field, a Southern Illinois politician, who at that time was secretary of state. They also passed through Belleville and this gave the Belleville Advocate an opportunity to hold them up to ridicule. The paper was violent in its criticisms. It referred to these two campaigners as "Missionaries Field and Lincoln." One expression will suffice, "These same missionaries were in Belleville last week, for the purpose of lecturing the besotted St. Clairmen for their obstinate adhesion to their sins. . ." There was no public speaking in either Alton or Belleville, only personal contact was engaged in on this visit.

Lincoln arrived in Alton, September 22, 1842, to measure broadswords with James Shields. They had come from Springfield, Lincoln by way of Jacksonville, White Hall, Jerseyville to Alton; while Shields had traveled to Alton by way of Hillsboro. Nobody was hurt in this duel, but Lincoln had lots of fun out of it.

March 27, 1849, Lincoln was in Alton for a short stay on his way home from the inauguration of President Taylor. This also was the end of his term in congress.

The Alton Courier on August 7, 1856, advertised Lincoln as one of the speakers in a great Fremont mass-meeting to be held in Alton, August 16, 1856. But Lincoln was not at this meeting; he was in Oregon in the north part of the state. The Courier may have been incorrectly informed as to Lincoln's speaking programme.

The Illinois state fair, which has always been an occasion for political round-ups, was held in Alton in the first week of October, 1856. Mr. Angle in his "Day by Day" says that the state fair, in progress at Alton, was the occasion for a large Fremont demonstration. Lincoln spoke in the afternoon to an audience gathered in front of the Presbyterian church. "He made, as he always does, an earnest, argumentative, patriotic and exceedingly able speech," writes Mr. Angle. After Lincoln's speech the meeting adjourned until evening, but Lincoln left for home on an early train.

The spring of 1858 was a busy time for Lincoln. He had a large amount of court work and the calls came thick and fast for his appearance in various parts of the state. Two pressing invitations came from Egypt. One was from J. F. Alexander of Greenville, who had just launched the Greenville Advocate to support Mr. Lincoln's candidacy for the United States senatorship. The other call was to help M. W. Delahay, a pronounced Buchanan follower, to carry out a sort of understanding between some of the Republicans and the leading Danites, having for its purpose to keep the Buchanan ticket in the field in order to weaken Douglas' cause here in Illinois. Lincoln and Delahay of Alton went from that city over to Edwardsville, May 18, 1858, where Lincoln made a rousing Republican speech. Mr. Delahay, though a Buchanan man, still appeared to be campaigning for Douglas, at least, he later came out for Lincoln.

Lincoln's last visit to Alton was probably October 15, 1858. This date in Alton was the seventh and last of the joint debates. Douglas and Lincoln debated in Quincy October 13th, and in Alton the 15th. The two candidates came down the river on the packet, *Louisiana,* and arrived in Alton early the morning of the 15th. Excursions on the river and from Springfield over the Chicago and Alton railroad brought large numbers, yet the attendance was not over 5,000, which was disappointing. Lincoln had for special guests at this meeting Mrs. Lincoln, Judge Trumbull, and John Hitt, a brother of the stenographer who was following

101

up the meetings. These guests, together with Horace White and Robert Hitt, all took dinner at the Franklin House that evening.

SALEM, JUNE 9 (?) 1849

Salem was founded in 1823, located on the old Vincennes-St. Louis trail which was made a United States mail route as early as 1805. For many years Salem was the principal town between Vincennes and St. Louis.

The author believes that Lincoln was in Salem at least on two occasions prior to his election to the presidency. The first of these two occasions was in 1849 when the public mind was agitated over the "State Policy" schemes, and the second time was in 1856, in the first state-wide Republican campaign waged by that party.

In 1849 the leading men of the state were divided into two groups—the supporters of the "State Policy" and the opponents of that policy. The "State Policy" was a doctrine that Alton should be made the western terminus of all rail-roads asking for charters from the Indiana line to the Mississippi river. There were many bitter opponents to this policy. These believed that good policy, indeed a much better policy, was to terminate these east and west roads at the Mississippi river at the site of the present city of East St. Louis.

On June 4-5, 1849, a monster meeting of four thousand self-appointed delegates, opponents of the "State Policy," assembled at Salem to create sentiment against the "State Policy" doctrine and to win to the cause of the opponents the members of the legislature. Zadoc Casey of Mt. Vernon presided over this great meeting and William Smith Waite of Greenville was the principal speaker for the opponents.

Lincoln had only recently returned from Washington at the end of his term as congressman from the seventh congressional district. He was very busy making preparations to return to the capital to press his claim for appointment

102

as commissioner of the general land office. His route lay through Terre Haute and Indianapolis in going, but on his return, immediately after Justin Butterfield had secured the appointment to the commissionership, Lincoln came by way of Clarksville, Chillicothe, Cincinnati, Louisville, Vincennes, and to Salem.

The great convention was over, but many prominent men were still actively canvassing the situation and Lincoln would have an opportunity of meeting many friends and thus get some knowledge of the direction of the current of public opinion.

It is generally known that Lincoln and the Reverend James Lemen of Monroe county were devoted friends. Rev. Benjamin Lemen, a member of this family, lived in Salem in the forties and fifties. Gold was discovered in California in 1848, and in the spring of the next year the gold rush swept many to the gold fields. The Rev. Lemen of Salem was caught in the westward current. He packed a cedar chest full of medicine, put his Bible in his pocket, bade good-by to family and friends and was soon digging gold and preaching to the Indians.

Mrs. Lemen was a lady cultured and resourceful. She conducted a seminary and kept roomers and boarders. When the stage driver from Vincennes approached Salem on a June afternoon in 1849, knowing that the hotels were crowded, he drove to the home of Mrs. Lemen where Lincoln found not only a room but a kindly welcome from a genuine hostess.

"Lincoln stayed over night in Salem at the home of Mrs. Benjamin Lemen which is located at what is now 321 S. Franklin Avenue," says Miss Helen MacMackin, State Regent of the Daughters of the American Revolution, and whose home is in Salem. "The stage driver knew that Mrs. Lemen had a room and so he took Lincoln there for the night."

WHEN LINCOLN CAME TO EGYPT

Lincoln took a very active part in the Republican campaign of 1856. Colonel William H. Bissell of Belleville was that party's candidate for governor. Lincoln and Bissell were fast friends. Lincoln brought about the nomination of Bissell and so was deeply concerned in his election. But most of Lincoln's time in the canvass was spent in the north part of the state. He came into Egypt only three times—once in September, once in early October, and again on October 18.

Elsewhere is a letter from Jesse K. Dubois urging Lincoln to come into the Wabash country for a day or so. Lincoln had previously promised to come about the middle of September. In reply to this plea from Dubois he said, "I will strain every nerve to be with you and him (Trumbull). More than that I cannot promise now."

Angle's "Day by Day" locates Lincoln in Vandalia on Thursday, September 18, on his way to the Wabash country. It also says that he spoke in the old state house on Tuesday, the 23rd. This gives Friday, Saturday, and Monday to be accounted for. The author believes Lincoln was in Albion on Friday, the 19th, in Lawrenceville on Saturday, and remained over Sunday with his friend Dubois, and was in Salem on Monday, the 22nd, and in Vandalia the 23rd. Angle says in a note that a big Republican rally was advertised for Salem for Monday, the 23rd, and that it is safe to assume that Lincoln spoke there at this time.

On this visit to Salem, Lincoln found accommodations at the hotel, the Salem House, kept by a Mr. Ray whose granddaughter, Mrs. Walter Cope, lives at Tonti, Illinois. Mrs. Cope remembers well hearing her grandfather tell about Lincoln's staying at his hotel. General James S. Martin, an honored citizen of Salem, was accustomed to tell of seeing Lincoln at the hotel on this occasion in a conference with leading Republicans. General Martin was a young Republican of prominence at this time and he was acquainted

104

with Lincoln. General Martin stated that Douglas was in Salem at this time and was a guest at the Park Hotel.

It would not be difficult to over estimate Lincoln's political popularity in Egypt in the campaign of 1856. In 1840 Lincoln had taken a very active part in the campaign in Egypt as a Whig. Now in 1856 he is a Republican, and it is very doubtful whether as a Republican he is as popular as he was as a Whig in 1840 and 1844. He appeared only three times as a Republican in Egypt in the Fremont campaign of 1856. First, this five-day dash into the Wabash country of which the Salem visit was a part, second, a visit to Alton October 2, at the state fair, where he delivered a patriotic address, and a third when he appeared at Belleville with Bissell, Trumbull, and Gillespie, October 18. Granted that Lincoln had not grown in favor with the masses, yet among the leading men of Egypt his stature is ever increasing.

SOME TRADITIONS

Tradition is history by word of mouth. Some people have a contempt for traditional stories. They forget that most matter called history was tradition before it was reduced to writing. It is not an easy task to blot out a tradition particularly if it is one of personal or family relations. Often such traditions persist even after proof has shown their falsity. Traditions may eventually be established as facts by indisputable evidence.

There are quite a few traditions about Lincoln's presence in Egypt. In his day there seems to have been but two good reasons for his coming into this region. One was the attendance upon the courts in the several county seats; the other to take part in political discussions. It is hard to conceive that he should have had any strictly business affairs that would have called him into Egypt. He had no social obligations that would have called him here. And it is doubtful if any form of religious duty could have caused his presence in Egypt.

Judge Thomas J. Layman of Benton says that back in the year 1855 a man by the name of William Dungy lived east of Benton in the country. Mr. Dungy had two letters which he had received from Lincoln relative to a suit he had about some real estate. Mr. Dungy would bring these letters with him when he would come into Benton, and often spent some time in the law office of Judge Layman's father. Whenever there was any excuse for doing so, he would show these

107

letters and thus make it appear that he and Lincoln were good friends.

Now Dungy was a Portuguese and very dark. He had married the sister of a Mr. Spencer. From some cause Spencer disliked his brother-in-law very much and often would speak very slightingly of him. One day Spencer said to a neighbor, "Bill Dungy was a damned negro." Of course, the neighbor told Dungy who sued Spencer, his brother-in-law, for slander. Abe Lincoln took Dungy's case. The verdict of the jury was $600.00 damage. (See Angle's "Day by Day," page 94.)

A traditional Lincoln story is reported by William N. Moyer of Mound City, Pulaski county, Illinois. Mr. Moyer is now along in the 80's and is well posted not only in the local traditional stories, but has made some very valuable research reports to the State Historical Journal. He tells this story as he got it from a justice of the peace in whom Mr. Moyer had confidence.

Between 1854 and 1858 Hiram Boren had the misfortune to take the life of another man. He was arrested and lodged in the jail in Caledonia, then county seat of Pulaski county. Mr. Boren had relatives in Springfield. He asked them if there was a good defense lawyer in that city. They replied that Abraham Lincoln was the best defense lawyer in the country. He was engaged to defend Mr. Boren.

Lincoln often rode horseback to towns where there was no railroad connection, but in reaching Caledonia he took the train for Decatur, then the Illinois Central to Cairo, and a boat up the Ohio sixteen miles to Caledonia. On opening the case, he found on the jury Joel Lackey, a friend whom he knew very well.

When the trial was over, Lincoln expressed a desire to reach the Illinois Central railroad so he might get an early train for Decatur. Now Joel Lackey lived a mile and a half east of the village of Pulaski, a station on the Illinois Central railroad, sixteen miles north of Cairo. It is six and a half miles from Caledonia west to Pulaski station, and five miles to the home of Joel Lackey. Mr. Lackey very generously invited Lincoln to go home with him and remain over night and on the morrow Mr. Lackey would be responsible for seeing that Lincoln caught the first train for Decatur.

Lincoln was very thankful for so generous an invitation. He accompanied Mr. Lackey and late that particular afternoon one might have seen Lackey, a hill farmer of Pulaski county, and Lincoln, the future President of the United States, riding merrily along the country road from Caledonia to the village of Pulaski with a strong oak board for the "seat-board" and a big sheep-skin for a cushion. Lincoln reached the station in time for the morning north-bound train for Decatur, and the kindly regard of Lincoln for the Lackeys was renewed and strengthened.

Joel Lackey had a brother, Alfred, who lived close by. The two brothers came from Tennessee in 1822 and settled in the hills five miles west of Caledonia. Each had a daughter and Joel had a son named Decatur. Decatur, Joel's son, and Alfred's daughter, Mrs. Lucinda Alred, lately deceased, always insisted that Lincoln once spoke at a religious gathering held in Joel's new double-log house which was built in 1850, or thereabouts. Mr. Moyer of Mound City, Mrs. Julius Schuh, and Mrs. Oscar L. Herbert of Cairo, and Mrs. Grace Cabot Toler of Mounds all say that the two cousins repeated this story to them in 1936 and vouch for the truthfulness of these witnesses.

W. T. Wooden, of Mt. Vernon, relates an incident which he has received through his great uncle, A. J. Tharp, who lived at Casey, seventeen miles west of Marshall in Clark county, Illinois. Lincoln was to speak at Marshall in a great campaign rally, presumably in 1844 when he was a candidate for elector on the Clay ticket. Mr. Tharp with team and wagon appropriately decorated conveyed a host of young ladies representing the states in the Union to Marshall to attend the afternoon rally.

When the rally was over, it was discovered that Lincoln would have to get a conveyance back to Casey where he was to speak at night. Arrangements were made with Mr. Tharp who gave Lincoln passage with the young ladies. Mr. Tharp said that he saw Lincoln at political gatherings several times after that and that Lincoln always recognized him and would speak of the jolly ride from Marshall to Casey.

G. L. Kenner of Mt. Carmel says his uncle, Alvin R. Kenner, was sheriff of Edwards county about 1840, and that he drove Lincoln over the county during his canvass of that section. One day they drove by a field where there was a persimmon grove. Lincoln observed the ripe persimmons and expressed a desire for them. Mr. Kenner was accommodating enough to get his hands full of the precious fruit which he gave to Lincoln.

A prominent lawyer of Benton, Illinois, tells that as Lincoln was returning to Springfield from attending court at Mt. Vernon, Illinois, the stage coach broke down a few miles out, requiring some time for temporary repairs. While waiting, Lincoln sauntered over to a farm house where he found the woman of the house doing her churning. He sat watching her and rested. She offered him a glass of fresh buttermilk which he drank. He then played with a small boy till the stage was ready to continue its journey.

THE BATTLE BEGINS

The first of the seven joint debates was held at Ottawa, LaSalle county, Illinois, August 21, 1858. It was estimated that there were 20,000 people present. The debate was quite fully reported in the local as well as in the metropolitan press. Senator Douglas in his first speech asked Lincoln seven questions which Lincoln answered later at the meeting at Freeport.

The second debate was held at Freeport in Stephenson county, August 27th, 1858. The attendance was estimated at 15,000. Ingalls Carleton, a resident of Freeport, who was interviewed in 1908 on the occasion of the fiftieth anniversary of the debate in that city, said, "Presently Lincoln and Douglas came out on the balcony together arm in arm and the crowd cheered and shouted. They just stood there and bowed." He said Douglas was well dressed, and that Lincoln was shabbily dressed in comparison with Douglas.

In the Freeport debate, Lincoln asked Douglas this question: "Can the people of a United States territory, in any lawful way, against the wish of any citizen of the United States, exclude slavery from its limits, prior to the formation of a state constitution?" If Mr. Douglas wishes to stand by his doctrine of 'Squatter Sovereignty' as laid down in the Compromise of 1850 and in the Kansas-Nebraska Act, he will say 'Yes.' If he says 'Yes,' he will make a bitter enemy of every slave holder and takes his stand against the Supreme Court's decision in the Dred Scott case. If he says 'Yes,' he loses the leadership of the united Democratic Party. If Mr.

111

Douglas says 'No,' he turns his back upon his oft-announced doctrine of Squatter Sovereignty, and will lose the Senator-ship in Illinois."

Senator Douglas said neither "Yes," nor "No." But he did say, "I answer emphatically as Mr. Lincoln has heard me answer a hundred times from every stump in Illinois, that in my opinion the people of any territory can by lawful means exclude slavery from their limits prior to the forma-tion of a state constitution....for the reason that slavery can not exist a day or an hour anywhere unless it is sup-ported by local police regulations."

The press and leaders in the South were greatly angered. Their attitude is well stated by Judge Judah P. Benjamin, senator from Louisiana, though he made the following state-ment two years later: "We accuse him (Senator Douglas) for this, to-wit: That having bargained with us on a point upon which we were at issue, that it should be a judicial point; that he would abide the decision; that he would act under the decision, and consider it a doctrine of the party; that having said that to us here in the senate, he went home, and under the stress of a local election, his knees gave way; his whole person trembled. His adversary (Lincoln) stood upon principle and was beaten; and lo! he is the candidate of a mighty party for the Presidency of the United States. But the grand prize of his (Douglas') ambition slips from his grasp because of his faltering—and his success in the canvass for the Senate purchased for an ignoble price, has cost him the loss of the Presidency of the United States."

HORACE WHITE, EDITOR CHICAGO TRIBUNE.

DOUGLAS EN ROUTE

No one it seems has worked out the whereabouts of Douglas after the joint discussions at Ottawa and Freeport. We may be assured, however, that he was very busy. General Linder in his "Bench and Bar" says that he was invited to accompany Senator Douglas in his canvass in Northern Illinois, but does not say that he was with him. But he does say that he accompanied the senator and Mrs. Douglas from St. Louis around on his Southern Illinois canvass at least as far as Charleston.

The files of the St. Louis Daily Herald for September, 1858, show that Senator and Mrs. Douglas were in St. Louis on the 9th and 10th of September and that on the 11th the senator went to Belleville from St. Louis on a special train of several coaches filled with Douglas enthusiasts. He spoke in Belleville on the 11th and also in Waterloo, fifteen miles to the southwest of Belleville. This was on Saturday. Whether he returned to St. Louis or proceeded to Chester, it is not definitely known.

The St. Louis Daily Herald in describing the senator's visit to that city referred especially to the fact that Mrs. Douglas was accompanying her husband on this journey to Jonesboro. The paper spoke very highly of Mrs. Douglas' beauty and grace, and commented on her value to the senator in his canvass.

General Linder says that John A. Logan joined the Douglas party at Chester on Monday, September 13, and that the senator, Logan, and himself all made speeches to

113

the people who had gathered in that city. That evening the party boarded the "James H. Lucas," a river steamboat, plying between St. Louis and Memphis, on their trip to Cairo, Illinois.

Tuesday morning this craft rounded the southern end of the peninsula on which Cairo stands and turned north into the broad and beautiful Ohio to unload its distinguished passengers at the gates of the metropolis of Egypt. If the photographs made by Brady, the Civil War photographer, are to be depended on, Cairo was not a very big city in 1858. A large reception committee of representative citizens, a fine brass band from Jonesboro, and a large body of interested people accompanied the senator, Mrs. Douglas, General Linder, and John A. Logan to the Taylor House. John A. Logan was the Democratic candidate for congress on the Douglas wing of the Democratic party. Jonesboro had been selected for the joint debate in Mr. Logan's district, which was the ninth.

In 1908, the fiftieth anniversary of the Jonesboro debate, there were many citizens in Cairo who remembered Douglas' visit to their city on his way to Jonesboro. Douglas was amongst his political friends in Cairo. Alexander county was torn asunder by the two factions of the Democratic party. The Douglas faction polled 322 votes in Alexander county in the November election while the Buchanan followers polled only 24 votes. However, the Cairo Weekly Times and Delta, a local newspaper, was bitter against Douglas, and it certainly was not mealy-mouthed about its criticisms of the senator and his factional friends.

From personal interviews with Cairo citizens and other dependable sources, the following facts were gleaned: A brass band from Jonesboro under the leadership of Professor Joseph E. Terpinitz, was engaged by the Douglas reception committee of Cairo. The reception committee consisted of Colonel Samuel Staats Taylor; S. S. Brooks; B. O. O'Shaughnessy; Colonel John S. Hacker; Captain Abe Williams; Captain Billy Williams; Mose Harrell, mayor of

WHEN LINCOLN CAME TO EGYPT

Mound City; John Q. Harmon; M. S. Ensminger; Henry H. Kandee; H. Too Aspern; Ed Willott, and others.

The distinguished guests, members of the reception committee, the band and visiting friends all proceeded to the Taylor House which was selected as the headquarters for the senator and Mrs. Douglas during their short stay in the city. The hotel was a three-story wooden building at the southwest corner of Fourth and Commercial Avenue.

After reaching the Taylor House, the band played a piece or two and the crowd soon dispersed. The chief thing on hand at this time was preparation for dinner. It had been agreed that some of the Democratic ladies of the city were to assist the cooks at the Taylor House to prepare the noon meal. This they did. Captain Billy Williams says he went to the Taylor House to pay his respects to the senator. After a few moments with Mr. Douglas he went into the kitchen to see how the dinner was coming on, and there he was introduced to Mrs. Douglas, who was busily engaged herself in making pies for the dinner.

The noon meal was a sort of social affair. In addition to the distinguished guests and the reception committee, there were Judge Josh Allen, John A. Logan, General Usher Linder, Honorable W. T. Dowdall, and a sprinkling of the gentler sex. Douglas spoke to a small gathering of the citizens at St. Mary's Park in the afternoon, and at night there was the social climax of the day, a big ball at the Taylor House. This affair was under the management of William A. Hacker, C. G. Simons, H. Watson Webb, with a good deal of help from Captain Billy Williams and Colonel Taylor. Senator and Mrs. Douglas led the Grand March after which Mr. Douglas retired for study and sleep. Mrs. Douglas danced with many of the prominent men.

In the summer of 1908, the fiftieth anniversary of the Lincoln and Douglas debate, the author spent some time in Cairo searching out those people who remembered the incidents of that now important day, September the 14th, 1858. He was fortunate to find quite a few men who recalled well

115

that interesting gathering. Among those who rendered valuable help in finding the old citizens were the county superintendent of schools, John Snyder, Mayor George Parsons,
Captain Billy Williams, and Attorney M. J. Howley. With
the help of these men, carpenters, hod carriers, merchants,
lawyers, and physicians were interviewed. There was common testimony about quite a few matters. All agreed that
Mrs. Douglas was a very cultured lady, beautiful and gra-
cious, that Senator Douglas showed the effects of a long,
hard campaign, that there may have been much interest but
a noticeable lack of enthusiasm, that there was a marked
absence of Egypt's public men, and that the visit of Senator
Douglas and Mrs. Douglas was a red letter day for the
young city.

Cairo was up and stirring betimes Wednesday morning, September 15, as a special train stood ready to take
people either to the state fair then on at Central City or to
the joint debate that day at Jonesboro. Attached to the
special train, was a flat car upon which was mounted a
small brass cannon manned by a volunteer group who knew
something of loading and firing artillery. Professor Terpinitz,
who had charge of the band, said the men fired the cannon
as they passed the villages or groups of people along the
way. He said the artillerymen worked hard as the train
passed through the foothills of the Ozarks.

There was not a very large crowd of people at the Anna
station when the Cairo special arrived and there was some
delay in getting the men and boys headed towards Jonesboro,
which is a mile down the road from Anna. Senator Douglas
and some friends probably dined at the Union Hotel in
Jonesboro that noon after their arrival.

Andrew J. Bunch, a young man learning the blacksmith trade at that time in Jonesboro, was asked to serve on
the Douglas reception committee. In 1908, he was about
seventy years old. When the author met him at that time and
asked him to tell what he remembered about the occasion of
the debate, he said: "Jonesboro was a small town of less

116

than a thousand people when Lincoln and Douglas visited it. There was a hotel on the east side of the square kept by a man by the name of Sheets, and another one on the west side kept by a Mrs. Williams. The courthouse in the center of the square was very dilapidated. There was no other floor than a dirt floor. The present courthouse was just being plastered. The prominent men of the community were Colonel John Hacker, his two sons, William and Henry, the latter being a doctor. William had been to West Point to school and he was very active in politics. Colonel John Dougherty was another very prominent man. His son, Lafayette, was the United States marshal for the southern district of Illinois. Other leading men were John E. Nail, William Bunch, Ephraim Kimmel, Willis Willard, John Greer, Adam Cruse, Dr. Toler, Joseph E. Terpinitz, John R. Miller, George Williams, Samuel Flagler, and Jeff Baldwin. Jonesboro was almost solid in its leanings toward Buchanan and it was a cold reception that Douglas got. There was a reception committee, but the Hackers and Dr. Toler were the main ones. Slight preparations were made for the debate. One reason was that the Buchanan people would not help in any way. The debate was held a quarter mile north of town. The Douglas cannon was taken to the grounds and placed on the southside and was fired several times while Douglas was speaking. When the speaking was over, some one called for Dougherty to speak and he came to the stand, but the confusion was too great and he gave it up. Josh Allen called for General Linder and he came forward and spoke. I do not know what became of Lincoln and Douglas after the speaking."

117

LINCOLN EN ROUTE

In 1908, Horace White who accompanied Lincoln on his speaking tours, described the route taken by Lincoln and himself from Freeport, where the second debate was held, to Jonesboro, the place of the third debate. Mr. White wrote from Palisades, New York, where he was temporarily residing, and doubtless wrote without his notes, but in the main he was correct. The following route is Mr. White's with corrections from "Lincoln Day by Day" by Paul Angle, secretary of the State Historical Library, Springfield, Illinois.

The Freeport debate was held on Friday, August 27, 1858. Lincoln passed through El Paso, 20 miles north of Bloomington, where he changed cars. An hour's wait here gave him an opportunity to make a short address. He reached Peoria that afternoon and remained over night. On Sunday he passed through Pekin and on Monday was in Tremont, Tazewell county, where he spoke to a Republican county convention. Tuesday, August 31, he and John M. Palmer spoke at a rousing Republican rally in Carlinville. On Wednesday, September 1st, he passed through Springfield and Decatur on his way to Clinton, Dewitt county, where he spoke on Thursday. On Friday, the 3rd, he was the guest of David Davis in Bloomington where he spoke the following day. Sunday, September the 5th, Lincoln spent with his family in Springfield. On Monday, September the 6th, he spoke in Monticello and on Tuesday at Mattoon and again later in the day at Paris. Here he met Owen Lovejoy, brother of the Alton martyr. He spent Wednesday and Thursday

119

and part of Friday getting from Paris through Shelbyville, Hillsboro, Alton, and to Edwardsville.

Saturday, September 11th, Lincoln was in Edwards-ville the guest of his dear friend, Judge Joseph Gillespie. He was now on Egyptian soil. Horace White says here was a meeting essentially different from other great rallies of this campaign. Judge Gillespie presided. There was great emotion 'manifest, and some of Lincoln's finest philosophy was broad-cast. At night he spoke to a German community at Highland.

Judson Phillips was the son of D. L. Phillips, who was the Republican candidate for congress against John A. Logan of Benton, the Democratic candidate, and John S. Hunsaker of Union county, the candidate on the Buchanan ticket. Judson Phillips was eleven years old in the summer of 1858 and had in 1908 a very vivid recollection of many details of that historic day, June 15, 1858. The author spent several hours with him in the summer of 1908 prior to the celebra-tion of the fiftieth anniversary of the Jonesboro debate.

Judson Phillips said that his father was land agent for the Illinois Central railroad and was away from home quite a deal of the time. On the 14th of September, the day before the debate in Jonesboro, his father met Lincoln in Centralia or Central City, and accompanied him to Anna. Mr. White and Mr. Hitt, newspaper correspondents, were with Lincoln. On arriving at Anna, Lincoln went to the home of Mr. Phillips which was the second house west of the Episcopal church on the main street, then (1908) occupied by Dr. Otrich.

Mr. Phillips said his father and Lincoln were good friends, and that he had heard his father say that Lincoln was averse to coming to Jonesboro for one of the joint de-bates. Lincoln explained that the fight in Egypt was between the two factions of the Democratic party, and that it would be a waste of time for Douglas and himself to discuss their differences in Jonesboro. But his father was very anxious to have Lincoln come and it was so arranged.

The town of Anna was only four years old in 1858 and

there were only a few dozen houses in the new town. Horace White, the secretary of the State Republican Committee and also the representative of the Chicago Press and Tribune, and Robert R. Hitt, the official stenographer for the same paper, were obliged to go over to the county seat town of Jonesboro, a mile west, and take lodging at the Union Hotel, a very large three-story building on the east side of the square.

After the evening meal, on September 14, Lincoln, Mr. Phillips, and the son, Judson, then eleven years old, went over to Jonesboro to visit with Mr. White and Mr. Hitt. They with others sat in front of the Union Hotel and ob-served Donati's comet which was giving free nightly enter-tainments in the southwest part of the heavens. Mr. White afterwards said that Lincoln was very much interested in the comet, and they all told what they understood a comet in the heavens meant. After a stay of an hour, the visitors returned to Phillips' home in Anna.

On the morning of the 15th, the day of the debate, Dr. McVane, a prominent Democrat who lived near D. L. Phillips, offered to take Lincoln and Mr. Phillips on a morn-ing ride through the Ozark hills. Dr. McVane was quite a horse fancier and drove a fine span of matched geldings. When they were ready to start the doctor asked the young Phillips boy if he would like to go with them and, of course, the youngster was glad of the chance, and thus Judson Phillips had an opportunity to become well acquainted with Abraham Lincoln.

They drove to the western part of the young village where there is presented a beautiful view of the Ozarks, through the hills to Old Jonesboro, out to the fair grounds where the debate was to be held, and thence west into the valley of Dutch creek, past the James Morgan home and the Cherokee Indian camp, through Dug Gap and out into the great alluvial plain of the Mississippi. Lincoln expressed a desire to get out of the carriage to get a better view of the great level valley of the river and the towering bluffs

121

which mark its eastern border. Judson said that all were out in a jiffy except Lincoln, for he had such a hard time getting his legs out of the carriage that he laughed at Lincoln's predicament. Judson said that Lincoln was greatly pleased with the view of the valley and the bluffs.

On returning to Jonesboro, Dr. McVane drove his friend Lincoln to the home of Dr. Henry Hacker as Lincoln wished to pay his respects to the Hacker family. Colonel John S. Hacker and two sons, William, a lawyer and politician, and Henry, who was a physician, were politically devoted friends of Senator Douglas, but at the same time admirers of Lincoln. Colonel Hacker had served with Lincoln in the legislature. In 1908 the author called upon Mrs. Henry Hacker who then lived in Jonesboro. She was then above eighty and was the only one left of the old Hacker family.

Mrs. Hacker said she remembered very well several events of the day of the debate. She did not go to the debate as she had to care for her six-weeks-old baby, but that both Lincoln and Douglas came to see her. She said that her family were friends of Lincoln and she was glad to see him. Asked about Lincoln, she said he was not so well dressed as Douglas who came later in the day, but that he was so kind and sympathetic that one could not help liking him. He remained only a few moments. Mrs. Hacker remarked that the Hackers were special friends of Senator Douglas, and she was happy to have him call at her home to see her. She said he was very well dressed, wore kid gloves and a tall hat. She thought he looked somewhat fatigued from his speaking and traveling. Descendants of the Hacker family are still represented in Jonesboro and Cairo.

Judson Phillips said while in Jonesboro Lincoln spent some time about the old courthouse and with the politicians at the Union Hotel. Mr. Phillips and Lincoln returned to the Phillips home in Anna for an early noon meal as the Douglas train was expected from Cairo before the noon hour. Horace White said he was at the Anna station when the Douglas train with its cannon arrived. There was not a large number on the train nor a very large crowd at the station. Senator Douglas and some friends found carriages waiting to convey them to the county seat at Jonesboro, one mile west, while the band, the cannon, and the citizens were expected to form a procession and march to Jonesboro. There was some trouble in getting the band to lead the way. Professor Terpinitz, the director, told the author that the band boys were tired, hungry, and sleepy and it was not an easy task to get them to march in an orderly manner over to Jonesboro. Finally the band got in position and led the way followed by the cannon and a goodly number of citizens carrying flags and banners brought up from Cairo on the Douglas special.

Two trains came into Anna on that Wednesday, one from the north from Central City, and another train from Cairo which brought Senator Douglas and his friends up from the south. The people who gathered around the speakers' platform that afternoon were residents of Jonesboro and Anna, those who came on the two trains, and those who came in from the countryside and other places on horseback or in wagons. Horace White, The Chicago Press and Tribune's representative, reported to the author in 1908, that as he sat in front of the Union Hotel in Jonesboro on the morning of the debate, the country people who came into the town were sitting in homemade chairs in rickety farm wagons drawn by ox-teams. This was quite a sight for Mr. White who had spent most of his life on the broad prairies of central and northern Illinois.

A community of Germans had settled near Jonesboro in an early day and that is the explanation of the presence in the county seat of a very fine jeweler and musician and withal a polished gentleman. The people called him Professor Terpinitz. He had previously organized a very fine band, the only one in all Egypt. This band was engaged by the Democratic party to furnish music for the Douglas reception in Cairo and for the debate in Jonesboro.

123

WHEN LINCOLN CAME TO EGYPT

Professor Terpinitz and the author were good neighbors back in 1908. He said that the band was marching from the square to the fair grounds about two o'clock in the afternoon, and as they ascended a slight hill in the road he looked to his left and among a goodly number of men and boys he observed a very tall, large, ungainly man walking along with his hands behind him, his head bent forward, apparently in deep meditation. He wore a long, light-weight coat that made little pretense of fitting. Professor Terpinitz said to some of his band boys, "Who is that strange looking man walking along in the path?" One of the band boys answered, "Why, that is Lincoln from Springfield who is going to debate with Douglas." There seemed to be no one specially with him, though friends may have been with him in front or in the rear.

Judson Phillips said he was under the impression that his father, Lincoln, and himself rode from Anna to the Union Hotel in Charley Barringer's hack, and that his father and Lincoln spent some time before the debate talking with Mr. Douglas and other politicians. He said he did not know how his father and Lincoln went from the hotel to the fair ground, but he had always heard that they walked. When the father got to the fair grounds, he hunted up Judson and made him sit on the platform. Judson reported that just before the speaking, William Hacker came to his father and said, "I'll introduce Senator Douglas and you will introduce Mr. Lincoln." And so they did. Judson got tired, slipped off the platform, and made his way home, he was not interested in politics.

Captain John P. Reese of Cobden was twenty-four years old in 1858. He and Judge Lewis rode horseback from Cobden to the fair grounds. He was a Buchanan Democrat. He said the debate did not create much interest, though people went, apparently out of curiosity. He was introduced to both Lincoln and Douglas. "As we were riding from the courthouse to the fair grounds, we passed Phillips and Lincoln walking along the pathway next to the fence. There were scores of people walking, and Lincoln was attracting no special attention."

Captain Reese said some roughnecks in a wagon with fiddles tried to drown out Lincoln when speaking. Senator Douglas got up and said: "My friends, I want you to listen to my friend, Mr. Lincoln. Any indignity toward Mr. Lincoln is an indignity toward myself. For while we differ in politics, I want to say there is no better man than Mr. Lincoln." Everything then quieted down and Lincoln turned to Mr. Douglas and said, "Never mind, Judge, I'll soon get their attention." Lincoln always referred to the senator as judge.

AT THE DEBATE

Few people who attended the Jonesboro debate were thoughtful enough, immediately after the occasion, to write out a description of the speakers' stand, the men who occu-pied it, and the crowd of people who milled about. At such an occasion people do not think of the interest the men and women of the future will have in the things and incidents they witness.

This is easily understood when we recall that the people present at the Jonesboro debate came to see two great men and they cared little for the commonplace things about them. Again it is no reflection on the good people, who made such meager preparations as were provided on the knoll at the edge of the fair grounds, to say the preparations were very simple if, in fact, not crude. There was no community fund to draw on for the purchase of even the simplest decorations.

There were no planed boards for a platform, but plenty of rough-sawed planks from the near-by saw-mills. No writer or observer has mentioned any decorations, and seats for the listeners were entirely absent, and even seats on the platform for distinguished guests were limited.

In interviewing men in 1908 who were present at the debate, the author found few who had given attention to the physical conditions. Captain John P. Reese of Cobden probably was as observing as any. He said: "After dinner people began to stir around, the band played a piece or two, and we all moved toward the fair grounds. There was no order in the procession, no one was in charge, every fellow

127

seemed to be taking care of himself. I rode to the grounds on horseback with several others so traveling. On the way to the grounds I remember we passed Mr. D. L. Phillips and Mr. Lincoln as they were walking along the path by the side of the road.

"The preparations at the grounds were very simple. There was a stand or platform built to a tree for one support, I think it was a walnut tree. There were no seats arranged for the audience at all. People stood about and listened till they got tired and then they changed their position. I think William Hacker introduced Senator Douglas and D. L. Phillips introduced Mr. Lincoln."

The following is taken from Dr. John McLean's "One Hundred Years in Illinois" by courtesy of the Illinois State Historical Library secretary, Paul Angle:

"Having heard a great deal about Lincoln and my people being partisans of his, I determined to see and hear him. Accordingly, on the day of the Jonesboro debate, I drove the twenty-five miles from our home to Du Quoin, the nearest town on the Illinois Central, and there took a train to Jonesboro. The place where the debate was held was a grove in the edge of town, and there was a large crowd of people out to hear the oratorical gladiators, as both men by that time had national reputations as public speakers. The crowd in attendance was distinctly a Douglas crowd, so partisan in character that Judge Douglas gallantly and patronizingly bespoke their most courteous behavior toward his opponent, who, he assured us, was a gentleman in every respect.

"As much as I admired Lincoln and the things for which he stood, his personal appearance and address were very disappointing. He was a very tall man, standing about six feet six inches in his boots. While Douglas was speaking, Lincoln sat in a chair that was rather low, and as his feet were drawn in well toward the chair his knees were elevated to such a height and at such a sharp angle that it gave him a ludicrous appearance; and as he sat there he had a sad,

HENRY EDDY, PIONEER SOUTHERN ILLINOIS EDITOR.

faraway look in his eyes that gave me the impression that he was grieving about something and paying no attention whatever to the argument and eloquence of Judge Douglas. When the judge finished and Lincoln was introduced, he began to rise out of that chair, it seemed to me, one section at a time, until finally he stood head and shoulders above those around him. If I had been disappointed at his appear' ance, I certainly was at his delivery, for he began his address in a high-pitched, treble voice, all out of proportion to his massive head and frame, and accompanied it with rather an awkward carriage and gesture; but as he warmed into his subject, I became unconscious of his appearance and his voice, in the realization that I was listening to a wonderful message from a great soul, as with unerring accuracy, he recalled every point Douglas had made and demolished it with his masterful logic. The Douglas supporters who had come to hear the 'Little Giant' (as they fondly termed him) lay out Lincoln, went home thinking, and those of us who stood with Lincoln went home dead-sure that we were right."

When the fiftieth anniversary of the Jonesboro debate was celebrated, the author found a goodly number in Cairo and about Jonesboro who heard the great debate. In 1908 quite a few people whom the author interviewed said they did not go to the debate because they were not interested. A house-carpenter who was working on a building very near where Senator Douglas walked up the levee from the boat at Cairo said he ceased working while the reception committee and the band were forming the procession, but when they started toward the hotel he went back to his task again and that was the last he saw of the distinguished visitors.

A plasterer in Jonesboro, putting the finishing touches on the new courthouse, did not cease his troweling to attend the debate though the speaking was only a short distance away.

But eighty-two years will have elapsed between the time of the Jonesboro debate and the middle of September, 1940, and few are left now who heard the two great men.

WHEN LINCOLN CAME TO EGYPT

Judge William T. Pace of Mount Vernon vividly recalls the occasion. He says he has a very distinct picture of the two men, how they looked and acted, but remembers better perhaps the roaring of the cannon.

Tillman Manus of Anna is now in his 105th year and says he remembers the occasion and the two men. He was born in Cannon county, Tennessee, April 9th, 1835. He came to Anna, after wandering in Texas, in time to work on the Illinois Central railroad before it was completed. He enlisted in the 109th Infantry April 15, 1862, was transferred to the 11th in 1863 and was mustered out July 14th, 1865. It appeared to the writer that Mr. Manus' memory was very good with regard to the long ago, but that he had difficulty in finding words to use in his conversation. He described rather clearly the running of the batteries at Vicksburg and the incidents concerning the meeting of Generals Pemberton and Grant. He seemed to think that Lincoln's life was in danger while he was in Anna and Jonesboro. Yet he could not explain why he thought so. He has always been a Democrat, but said he was for Lincoln because Lincoln was in favor of sending the Negroes back to Africa. Mr. Manus gets about with considerable ease, has good appetite, sleeps well, and has one desire now—to live to be 105 years old.

THE DEBATE

Douglas Opens

Introductory

Note—Paragraphs numbered thus (8)

Two old political parties—Whig and Democratic. Their functions. Effort to abolish these two old parties; results in sectionalization. (1)

The two old parties united to postpone consideration of a vital question—slavery. This postponement secured through Compromise of 1850. The compromise measures rested on the people's right of self-determination. (2)

Was that principle, State Sovereignty, right or wrong? Union Whigs and Union Democrats said yes. Abolitionists and Southern Disunionists said no. The Whig and the Democratic National Conventions endorsed the Compromise. The Whigs claimed credit because Clay, the father of the Compromise, was a Whig; but the Democrats furnished twice as many votes in congress as the Whigs. (3)

Both great political parties in 1852 were pledged to support the Compromise. The Whigs since 1852 have become a sectional party; the Democratic party is still a national party. An appeal to all factions to rally under the Stars and Stripes and the Union. (4)

What has produced factionalism? Ambitious men have tried to organize an Abolition party. Great leaders are giving more attention to negroes than to whites. New York state has led the way. Hence a North and a South. (5)

WHEN LINCOLN CAME TO EGYPT

Lincoln has led the Whigs and Trumbull has led the Democrats into the abolition camp. As a reward for this betrayal, Lincoln was to have Senator Shield's place in the senate and Trumbull was to have Senator Douglas' place. (6)

A joint crusade throughout the state. They adopted an elaborate appeal to the north third of the state—Wilmot Proviso doctrine for all territory, no more slave states admitted, Fugitive Slave law abolished, slave trade between the states abolished, etc. (7)

The Republicans or Abolitionists in the North became Anti-Nebraskans in the Center, and Free Democrats in the South. In the North they brought Fred Douglas into the campaign, in the Center they used Lincoln, Lovejoy, Trumbull, and Breese. (8)

Criticises and condemns Trumbull, Wentworth, Reynolds, Breese, and Dougherty for entering conspiracy to wreck the Democratic party. Emphasizes change of principles in North, Center, and in the South. (9)

Why can't they have the same principles all over the state? Our political faith ought to be as broad, liberal, and just as the constitution. (10)

They change colors for partisan effect—to break down democracy. They succeeded in defeating Senator Shields. Praises military service of Shields. (11)

How was Trumbull elected? The discordant elements joined on abolitionism. Their creed was written by Lovejoy. Trumbull broke his pledge and Lincoln was defeated. (12)

Proof cited—reads extract from letter from Colonel James H. Matheny of Springfield. (13)

Describes confusion of the conspirators. But Lincoln was held in the alliance and now appears, claiming Douglas' seat in the senate. (14)

Shows agreement between Lincoln and the state convention of 1858. Shows Browning, Bissell, Williams, Wentworth, and Palmer all rejected for Lincoln. (15)

Ridicules the situation where there is only the possibility of one leader. (16)

"The House Divided" Speech

Shows Lincoln anticipated the nomination, hence a pre-pared speech. Reads part of speech. (17)

Quotes Lincoln as meaning government cannot stand as it was made by the fathers. Lincoln says to the South, "You must invade the North," and to the North, "You must invade the South." Either the South must abolish slavery or the North must adopt it. (18)

Warfare is the inevitable result. What good would come of this warfare? Shall there be unity in local and domestic institutions? Nature was not so ordered. (19)

Says that Lincoln means that the union of free and slave states is like a house divided against itself which is con-trary to God's law. When did he learn that this government is contrary to the law of God and cannot stand? Shows that the government has stood all these years and has grown in area and population. This is under a constitution which is contrary to the law of God. (20)

Says Lincoln is wiser than the men who framed the government. Says forefathers knew that uniformity in nature in different states did not exist, neither could our institutions. Government founded on diversity not on uniformity. (21)

DRED SCOTT DECISION

Douglas has no war to make on the supreme court. This court is the highest tribunal on earth. Its decisions are the law of the land. (22)

Lincoln objects to the Dred Scott decision because it deprives negroes of the rights of citizenship. The negro is not and never ought to be a citizen of the United States. The Almighty never made the negro capable of self-government. Lincoln follows Lovejoy who says the negro is endowed with right of equality with white men. (23)

133

WHEN LINCOLN CAME TO EGYPT

Writers and signers of the Declaration of Independence did not include negroes when they said all men were equal. If they did, then they should have freed their slaves. (24)

POPULAR SOVEREIGNTY

We ought to extend every right the negro is capable of enjoying, consistent with the good of society. Each state must decide what these rights are. Some states have already done so. Each state must leave that matter to every other state to settle for itself. (25)

Kentucky has settled that matter. I am opposed to the negro having the right of suffrage. The supreme court says a state may confer that right on any one. I am not going to make war on New York if she confers that right. (26)

Maine has conferred the right to vote upon the negro. (27)

Interprets the Dred Scott decision as saying that each state must settle its own problems along that line. Judge Taney lays down this doctrine. I accept it as law. (28)

The Union can endure forever—free and slave—if each state will carry out the principles upon which it was founded—if we live up to the principles of state sovereignty. When we take Cuba, we must let the people living there decide the question of slavery for themselves. (29)

The objection to the Lecompton Constitution was that it was not the will of the people living in Kansas. (30)

LINCOLN REPLIES

REBUTTAL

Lincoln agrees with Douglas in the doctrine that states have the right to do as they please about all their domestic affairs including that of slavery. Lincoln says he has no inclination to interfere with any state's domestic affairs, but Douglas placed him improperly relative to this matter. (1)

Douglas asks, "Why can't this Union endure permanently, half slave—half free?" Lincoln asks, "Why can't we let it stand as our fathers placed it?" The way our fathers left slavery, it was destined to ultimate extinction. Our fathers would have prohibited its entrance into new territories. Douglas and his friends have abandoned that policy. (2)

Brooks (who attacked Sumner) said, "Nobody expected slavery to last until this day." Judge Douglas and his northern slavery friends have never thought as did Brooks. They say the cotton gin will perpetuate it and nationalize it. (3)

Judge Douglas is helping to perpetuate it and nationalize it. (4)

Douglas says that once the policy of congress was to sectionalize it. He saw no desire to maintain that policy and he was helping to readjust it. Read his speech March 22nd for his policy. He has changed the policy of our fathers. (5)

Lincoln says that the judge's story about a contract between Judge Trumbull and himself is utterly false. Judge Douglas has no proof. Lincoln thinks that Mr. Matheny did

135

start this story about the contract. It was immediately denied by Judge Trumbull and myself. (6)

Lincoln says Judge Douglas is right about the Whigs and the Democrats recognizing the Compromise of 1850 as a finality. (7)

LINCOLN'S ARGUMENT

Compromise of 1850

The Compromise of 1850 did not repeal the Missouri Compromise of 1820. Judge Douglas was the chairman of the committee on territories. He brought in a bill to organize two territories. This bill repealed the Missouri Compromise. This bill started the slavery discussion. Why did he not let the slavery question alone? Why could not Kansas and Nebraska come in as did Iowa? Why, when we had peace under the Missouri Compromise, could you not let it alone? (8)

The Springfield speech, "A house divided against itself cannot stand," seems to worry the judge. I did not accept the nomination for senator. (9)

Douglas argues that variety in climate, soil, etc., necessitates variety in institutions. Lincoln agrees. No trouble has ever come from these facts. Louisiana's sugar plantations have never disturbed the people of Illinois. These differences are the cements of the Union. (10)

But not so with slavery. We have always had peace till an effort was made to spread it over more territory— new territory. Thus in 1820, and again when Texas applied for admission, at the close of the Mexican war, and in every move made in its behalf it has brought on agitation and resistance. Will the same cause which produced agitation in 1820, in 1845, in 1850, in 1854 cause agitation and resistance today? When will political agitation about slavery cease? (11)

It will cease when slavery is put back where it was originally or when it has spread all over the whole United States. (12)

WHEN LINCOLN CAME TO EGYPT

Judge Douglas charges that the Republicans in Illinois have three platforms—one for the North, one for the Center, and one for the South, and asks, "Why can't you come out and make an open avowal of principles in all places alike?" Douglas stands on a platform made in Springfield, April 22, but Colonel Dougherty stands on a platform made the 9th of June. Why can't there be uniformity? (13)

Is the judge willing for me to stand on the platform of June 16th? One cannot be responsible for the opinions of his friends. The judge agrees. (14)

SOME DEMOCRATIC RESOLUTIONS

Why then does he go about hunting up resolutions five and six years old and saying they are my platform? Lincoln says he'll try that on the judge. (15)

In 1850 a political friend of the judge by the name of Thomas Campbell ran for congress in the Galena district, and was elected on a platform the judge would not endorse. In answer to a series of questions, Campbell said that he would vote to abolish slavery in the District of Columbia, would oppose the admission of any more slave states, and would vote to repeal the Fugitive Slave Law. The judge would not endorse that platform. (16)

At the end of his term in congress, Mr. Campbell was given a good appointment. He is in this campaign helping to re-elect Judge Douglas.

Again a Dr. Moloney ran in the Joliet district on the Democratic ticket on a platform which said: "Resolved, That we are uncompromisingly opposed to the extension of slavery." Dr. Moloney said he would vote to abolish slavery in the District of Columbia, and oppose the admission of any more slave states. He was appointed to a civil office at the end of his term. At Naperville the Democratic Convention "Resolved, That in the opinion of this convention, the time has arrived when all men should be free, white as well as others." (17-22)

Judge Mayo in DeKalb favors Judge Douglas. He edits

a paper. In it he writes: "Our education makes us favor the equality of the blacks, that is, that they should enjoy all the privileges of the whites where they reside. We were brought up in a state where blacks voted and it never produced any trouble. We have seen many a 'nigger' that I thought more of than some white men." And yet this man is for Judge Douglas. The judge is not responsible for what this man says, but as much so as I am for some things my friends say. The Democratic state convention of Vermont, the judge's home state—"Resolved, That no more slave states should be admitted into the Federal Union." (23-26)

INTERROGATORIES

At Freeport Lincoln answered seven questions which Judge Douglas had asked at Ottawa. Lincoln then asked four questions, the second of which was, "Can the people of a United States territory, in any lawful way, against the wish of any citizen of the United States, exclude slavery from its limits prior to the formation of a state constitution?" The judge says they can in this way—first, by refusing to make laws to protect slavery; secondly, by enacting unfriendly legislation. (27-31)

The supreme court has declared that any congressional prohibition of slavery in the territories is unconstitutional, the constitution recognizes property in slaves, and that no person shall be deprived of property without due process of law. The constitution guarantees property in slaves in the territories. It would be the duty of the United States courts to protect the citizen in his right in the territory. (32)

Douglas stated in the Congressional Globe, June 9th, 1856, that the matter of holding slaves in a territory was a question for the courts, now he says it is a matter for the people of the territory. (33)

The theory that slavery can not enter a territory without police regulation is historically false. Slavery was originally introduced without police protection; Dred Scott was held in Minnesota without police protection. (34)

138

WHEN LINCOLN CAME TO EGYPT

Could the United States courts protect slavery in a United States territory? (35)

The legislator's first duty is to swear that he will support the constitution of the United States and the laws passed in pursuance thereof. Do you support the constitution by withholding needed legislation; much worse do you support it when you enact unfriendly legislation? (36)

Is not congress obligated to give legislative support to any right established under the constitution? Why must a conscientious congressman vote for a fugitive slave law? Because the constitution establishes the right of the owner of a slave to reclaim his property. (37)

Lincoln quotes the clause in the constitution giving owners of slaves the right to reclaim them if they are fugitives from service. This right is no better fixed than the one to hold slaves in territory of the United States. The first is fixed by the constitution, the second by the decision of the supreme court. Both the supreme law of the land. (38)

Fifth interrogatory—If the slave-holding citizens of a United States territory should need and demand congressional legislation for the protection of their slaves in such territory, would you, as a member of congress, vote for or against such legislation? (39-42)

Lincoln thinks the judge may say that he does not know that the supreme court has said that the territorial legislature cannot exclude slavery—Lincoln says they have decided only jurisdiction and this case is extra-judicially decided, as was the case that the Missouri Compromise was null and void. If congress cannot exclude slavery from a territory, neither can a territorial legislature. (43)

PERSONAL MATTERS

Lincoln quotes the judge's speech at Joliet about Lincoln's friends carrying him off the platform at Ottawa. He asks the judge why he did not tell the truth about it. Lincoln says he spoke six days between Ottawa and Freeport—and was not "laid up seven days."

139

WHEN LINCOLN CAME TO EGYPT

"Did the judge talk of trotting me down to Egypt to scare me to death? Why, I know this people better than he does. I was raised just a little east of here. I am a part of this people."

Lincoln closes—"I do not want to quarrel with him— to call him a liar—but when I come square up to him I don't know what else to call him if I must tell the truth out."

DOUGLAS CLOSES

Douglas explains reference to Lincoln's being carried from platform. It was said in playful manner. Indications are that Lincoln was angry. (1)

Douglas complains that Lincoln does not answer his questions—does not play fair in the game. Insists principles in northern congressional platforms same as Lovejoy's resolutions at Springfield. (2)

Cited the question, "Would you vote to admit a slave state if the people wanted slavery?" Lincoln did not answer "yes" or "no." (3)

Douglas thinks the senate a dangerous place for Lincoln with his attitude toward slavery. (4)

Lincoln charged with refusing to answer questions with reference to slavery. Douglas severe in his comments. (6)

Douglas cites Matheny that there was a bargain. States that other witnesses may be had. (7)

Lincoln charged with being unwilling to stand responsible for his party's platforms. Douglas admits waywardness of Campbell and Moloney. (8)

Douglas explains conversion of people of Chicago in 1850. (9)

Lincoln charged with not supporting his party's candidates, Lovejoy, Farnesworth, Washburne. Douglas insists that the Republican house is divided against itself. The North end against the Center and the South end. (10)

Calls attention to Lincoln's days in Indiana and Kentucky. Douglas calls Lincoln an Abolitionist and says Lincoln tries to cover it up by reference to his birth, and boy-hood in Kentucky and Indiana. (11)

Douglas describes his home in Vermont. Tells of re-ceiving the LL. D. degree. (12)

Douglas tells more of his early life. (13)

Cites Lincoln's question about congressional help in a territory. Answers by saying the Democratic creed would answer by saying no interference by congress. (14)

Douglas says that if a territory has population enough for a slave state, it has enough for a free state. (15)

Charges that Lincoln will not or cannot answer his own questions. (16)

Asks Mr. Lincoln if one is not bound by a decision which he objects to as much as one he agrees with. Courts are created to bind people to certain action. (17)

Douglas shows that Judge Taney places slave property on the same footing as any other property. Points out that local legislation is necessary and that it will drive out liquor or slavery. (18)

The Dred Scott decision cannot force slavery on a ter-ritory. (19)

THE DEPARTURE

The presence in the hill-town of the Ozarks of two great political leaders, one of whom was destined to take high rank among the great men of the earth, seems not to have appealed to the senses nor to have stirred the imagination of the public men of Egypt, to say nothing of the simple, common, honest folk that Horace White saw coming into Jonesboro the morning of the debate. All who have testified have given a common report, that there was considerable interest shown, but there was a lack of real enthusiasm. There was no high nervous tension and hence the relaxation was easy and harmless.

Senator Douglas returned to Cairo that same afternoon after the debate. It is doubtful whether the Senator's private car was used in making the trip from Cairo to Anna that morning. A regular train on the Illinois Central south-bound that afternoon would accommodate the Senator and his friends in returning to Cairo. There is slight evidence that Mrs. Douglas attended the Jonesboro debate. She had been very busy a day and an evening in Cairo in a political as well as in a social way, and to a lady of Mrs. Douglas' social experiences in Washington, the social attractions in the Jonesboro trip were insufficient to beguile her from a day of rest in the quiet old river city of Cairo.

It is known that Lincoln remained over night in Anna, the guest of Phillips. After the evening meal, Judson said Lincoln and his father sat on the porch and talked, and that a goodly number of neighbors came in for a few moments'

143

visit with them. All understood that tomorrow everybody was going to the state fair at Central City, and it was agreed that they retire early and arise early.

On Thursday morning Mr. and Mrs. Phillips, son Judson, and Lincoln were up early and soon on their way to the railroad station for it was conjectured that the good seats on the special train would be at a premium. The people were gathering and when it was stated that Senator Douglas' private car would be attached to the train, all was excitement. The train arrived and sure enough there was the senator's private car. There was a rush to see the car and to get a glimpse of the Senator and Mrs. Douglas. Judson said, "When we got started, Lincoln, who was riding in the day coach, was told that Senator Douglas was in the back car and he got up and said he would go and see him, but he immediately changed his mind and remarked, 'I guess I'll not bother the judge,' and sat down in the seat with L. W. Ashley and they sat and talked." Mr. Ashley was the chief civil engineer for the railroad for the Central City to Cairo division. Lincoln was attorney for the road and doubtless they knew each other. Judson says, "We were at the fair all day and at night mother and I took the train for home."

Judson remembered many things he saw at the fair, especially the sensational balloon ascension about which such a tragic story is told.

Professor Wilson made daily afternoon ascensions at the fair. It was the chief feature of the day. On Friday, the last day, he went up as usual and the brisk September breeze took him adrift toward the southeast in the direction of Mt. Vernon. After a several mile journey he descended near a farm house, securely anchored, as he thought, his half deflated balloon and was invited in to eat supper with the surprised farmer. There were two little children at the home, a boy four years and a girl of six. They were full of excitement and surprise and did not go in the house, but remained in wonderment near the big swerving balloon tugging at anchor. By some means they crawled into the basket. The big gas bag broke loose from its moorings just as the folks came to the door and discovered the balloon rising into the heavens. The balloon disappeared into the night with its helpless human cargo aboard. All night long the frantic search went on, but no signs of the balloon were to be found.

Early the next morning, a farmer, known as Squire Atkinson, residing in Moore's Prairie, the most southern township in Jefferson county, went to feed his stock. He saw a curious, curtain-like thing swinging from the top of a tree. It was the fugitive balloon. Neighbors were summoned and from the basket, safe and sound, the little boy and girl were rescued, hungry but wiser and none the worse off for their wild all night ride through the sky.

Judson said he saw Lincoln once after that day at the fair. "My father had a land office at Pana," he said, "and I was there with him. One evening late Lincoln came over from Decatur and stayed all night with father. He and father sat and talked so long that I got so sleepy I could not sit up any longer. They were talking about Mr. Lincoln running for the presidency. Presently Lincoln said, 'This boy is getting so sleepy, we had better go to bed!' We all three had to sleep in one bed. Lincoln was undressed and in bed first. I was standing near the foot of the bed, and when Lincoln pulled the cover up around his shoulders and straightened out his legs, his feet and ankles shot out a foot beyond the cover and the bed. It scared me and I yelled, making Lincoln laugh. Then we all laughed, and Lincoln, pulling his legs up under the cover, said, 'When I go to bed, I have to shut up like a jack-knife.' "

On the morning of the 16th the special from Cairo carrying Senator Douglas' private car reached Tamaroa. Judge Thomas J. Layman of Benton, Illinois, in a letter of May 1, 1912, to the author wrote:

"I am in receipt of your letter of April 24th, asking for some data relative to the visit of Stephen A. Douglas to Benton, September 16th, 1858. The

145

Benton Standard was burned three years ago and all the files of the paper since 1849 were destroyed. So I will not be able to give you much information.

"On the morning of September 16, 1858, Tillman B. Cantrell, Daniel Mooneyham, and other prominent citizens met Douglas at Tamaroa. At that time no railroad entered Benton. Douglas arrived at Benton some time before noon, and was taken at once to the home of John A. Logan on South Street. The old house where he was enter-tained is still standing. (But has since burned). He spoke in a grove in the northwest part of the town.

"The afternoon of the 15th, Mrs. John A. Logan went over the town and collected money to buy materials with which to make a flag. She and a party of women spent nearly all the night making the flag which was used in the procession and on the speaker's stand the next day. After Douglas had finished his speech he was driven back to Tamaroa and took the north-bound Illinois Central. I am told that John A. Logan presided as chairman of the meeting.

"Mrs. Tabitha Browning of this place has given me most of the information that I have ob-tained. I have been unable to find any one from Benton (besides John A. Logan) who attended the Jonesboro debate. W. S. Cantrell says that Judge M. C. Crawford of Jonesboro can probably tell you of the Benton visit of Douglas. If I find any thing further I will let you know. With best wishes, I remain,

"Very sincerely,

"Thos. J. Layman."

It is said that Douglas spoke briefly on the streets of Centralia on the evening of the 16th.

WHEN LINCOLN CAME TO EGYPT

There was more or less rivalry between Central City and Centralia. They were only a mile or so apart. The former the more important as a railroad point. Central City, with the fair as an attraction, could hold the crowds through the day, but at night Centralia, with blazing bonfires and playing bands and public speaking, drew the crowds. Henry C. Whitney, a lawyer-friend of Lincoln, and D. L. Phillips were constant attendants upon Lincoln till the arrival of his train for Mattoon at midnight. Mr. Whitney wrote of the incident the following in 1865:

"Lincoln and I were at the Centralia fair the day after the debate at Jonesboro. Night came on and we were tired, having been on the fair grounds all day. We were to go north on the Illinois Central railroad. The train was due at midnight, and the depot was full of people. I managed to get a chair for Lincoln in the office of the superintendent of the railroad, but the small politicians would intrude so that he could get scarcely a moment's sleep. The train came and was filled instantly. I got a seat for Lincoln and myself near the door. He was worn out and had to meet Douglas the next day at Charleston. An empty car, called a saloon car, was hitched on to the end of the train and locked up. I asked the conductor, who knew Lincoln and myself well, (we were both attorneys for the road) if Lincoln could not ride in that car; but the conductor refused. I afterwards got him in by a stratagem. At the same time George B. McClellan in person was taking Douglas around in a special train; and that was the unjust treatment Lincoln got from the Illinois Central railroad. Every interest of that road and every employee was against Lincoln and for Douglas."

A SHORT SAD CAREER

The series of joint debates closed with the Alton meeting, October 15, 1858. The election occurred November 2. It was soon known that the legislature was Democratic and therefore Douglas would be elected to succeed himself as United States senator. The short term of congress began in December, but Douglas knew that there was bitter opposition to him in congress and also among the southern people, and he thought it wise to attempt to regain their support by a visit to the South before appearing in congress.

He accordingly planned a speaking tour of the South, with a few weeks rest in the West Indies, and a tour of the eastern cities. He was kindly received wherever he appeared in public.

He arrived in Washington and took his seat in the senate January 10, 1859. He did not take part in the discussions for some time, for Douglas could easily see that his reception was lacking in cordiality. He must have felt keenly the loss of his position of leadership. In the early days of the session, before his return to Washington, he had been removed from the chairmanship of the committee on territories, a position which he had held for several years, and a position of honor to Senator Douglas.

The southern leaders in the senate, Green of Missouri, Davis of Mississippi, Mason of Virginia, Benjamin of Louisiana, Brown of Mississippi, and the President, Mr. Buchanan, began a war on Senator Douglas. They seemed to have one of two ends in view. First, to win him over

149

to their view as to the rights of slave holders in the territories; and second, failing in that, to crush out of him all ambition relative to the Democratic nomination for the presidency. Senators Green, Davis, and Benjamin were very active in their attacks on their colleague. In these running discussions both Mr. Douglas and his opponents were looking forward to the presidential election in 1860.

Senator Douglas was ambitious; he desired the Democratic nomination for the presidency in 1860. But he could not see any hope of obtaining it without the help of the southern states. The people of the free states were divided between the supporters of the newly organized Republican party and the old Democratic party. It appeared to be, as it later turned out to be, a three-cornered conflict. Douglas' problem, as a shrewd politician, was to hold the loyalty of the Democratic party of the North and win back in some way the alienated South.

The national Democratic convention met in Charleston, South Carolina, April 23, 1860. Two platforms were presented, one supporting the Douglas theory of state sovereignty, while the second supported the Dred Scott theory. The Douglas platform was adopted and eight southern states immediately withdrew and organized a convention of southern delegates. The main group of delegates voted fifty-seven times without making a nomination and adjourned to Baltimore. Douglas was nominated at Baltimore as the Democratic candidate for the presidency. The rump convention nominated John C. Breckenridge of Kentucky for President.

Douglas engaged actively in the campaign in his own behalf. He labored earnestly till election day though it was believed that he could easily see the final outcome. Douglas returned to his place in the senate. The session was full of trials and danger. The southern states were seceding, and treason was rampant in high and lowly official positions.

Douglas sounded the danger signal. He denied the right of secession, and supported the doctrine that the general government has the right to enforce its laws in every state.

WHEN LINCOLN CAME TO EGYPT

He was an honored guest on the fourth of March, 1861, and held Lincoln's hat while the President delivered his inaugural address.

He returned to Springfield where he spoke before the Illinois legislature. Here he denounced secession, and announced his loyalty to the Union, and pledged sacredly his support of President Lincoln. He left immediately for his home in Chicago, where, in the great Wigwam, before a great concourse of fellow citizens, he delivered his farewell address.

In this last public address he said: "There are only two sides to the question. Every man must be for the United States or against it. There can be no neutrals in this war; only patriots and traitors....I express it as my conviction before God, that it is the duty of every American citizen to rally around the flag of his country."

On his death-bed, when asked what message he wished carried to his sons, he replied, "Tell them to obey the laws and support the constitution of the United States."

LINCOLN MEMORIAL, FAIRFIELD, ILLINOIS.

A TRAGIC ENDING

Lincoln had arranged for Mrs. Lincoln to come down from Springfield to be present at the last debate at Alton. A letter to the author from John Hitt, a brother to Robert R. Hitt, the Press and Tribune's shorthand reporter, dated Chicago, July 25, 1908, says after the Alton debate was over that Horace White, Senator Lyman Trumbull, Robert R. Hitt, Mr. and Mrs. Lincoln, and himself all had an eve-ning meal at the hotel. John Hitt says in this letter, "I seem to hear Mr. Lincoln questioning Senator Trumbull whether he thought the meeting was productive of good, and spoke of the undemonstrative fashion the audience displayed in listening to the speeches of the day."

Following the Alton debate, Lincoln continued with a vigorous canvass in the northern parts of the state. He was not full of hope yet he was not discouraged. After the elec-tion, he said to a friend, "The cause of civil liberty must not be surrendered at the end of one or even one hundred defeats." Lincoln had really become a very successful lawyer and he could now easily find employment and success if he wished to continue in that calling. The fact is that he felt obliged to build up his financial resources.

But Lincoln had become a national figure and his time and his talent, many felt, belonged to the cause of humanity. The metropolitan press had done much to spread far and wide the logic, the power, and the honesty of this new western, country lawyer. Invitations came to him thick and fast from the East to deliver addresses on the public questions of the day.

The Democrats of Ohio in 1859 had called into their political canvass Senator Douglas, who had spoken in important places in that state. The Republicans of Ohio felt that Lincoln was the one who should be chosen to answer the brilliant senator. Lincoln therefore agreed to deliver at least two speeches in that state. On September 17, 1859, he appeared at Columbus where he delivered a telling speech with Senator Douglas' recent magazine article as the basis of attack. This Columbus speech and the Cooper Union address in New York without doubt helped largely to put Lincoln in the running for the Republican nomination for the presidency in 1860. On the day following the Columbus address, he spoke in Cincinnati.

The Republican party put out in printed form the joint debates between Douglas and Lincoln in Illinois, and Lincoln's two addresses in Ohio, as a powerful campaign document. But probably the most important public appearance of Lincoln prior to his election to the presidency was before a brilliant audience in the great Cooper Union in New York City in February, 1860. Herndon states that Lincoln, as well as his friends, felt doubtful of his being able to meet the demands of an eastern audience. But there was no doubt after the Cooper Union speech. William Cullen Bryant presided and introduced Lincoln. The audience, the subject, and the opportunity seemed to inspire the "rail-splitter from the Sangamon" and Lincoln surpassed himself in strategic attack, clearness of insight, power of logic, and brilliance of oratory.

He was now the most prominent political figure before the American people. "The country was amazed at the rare moral and intellectual character of Lincoln. . . . The homely story (of his life) gave a touch of mystery to the figure which loomed so large," Tarbell's Life of Lincoln, Volume II, page 127.

In May, 1860, Lincoln was nominated as the Republican candidate for the presidency. He was selected from among a large group of eminent Americans—Salmon P. Chase of Ohio; David Davis of Illinois; David Wilmot of Pennsylvania; William M. Evarts of Massachusetts; Gideon Welles of Connecticut; Joseph Medill of Illinois; Joshua R. Giddings of Ohio; Edward Bates of Missouri; Edwin M. Stanton of Ohio; William H. Seward of New York; Horace Greeley of New York. Five of these became members of President Lincoln's cabinet.

The days between Lincoln's election and his inauguration were busy days. He must select his cabinet, determine his position as to the government's attitude toward the seceding states, and prepare his inaugural address. His departure from Springfield for Washington was a sad farewell.

In his inaugural address, Lincoln repeated a formerly stated principle: "I have no purpose, directly or indirectly, to interfere with the institution of slavery in the states where it exists. I believe I have no lawful right to do so, and I have no inclination to do so."

Lincoln selected a strong cabinet. The members, however, did not always agree among themselves nor with Lincoln. But all problems, domestic and international, were happily solved. The war lingered till the President found the "silent man" who was willing "to fight it out on this line if it takes all summer."

As Commander-in-chief of the Army, Lincoln issued the Emancipation Proclamation giving freedom to all slaves held in territory then in rebellion against the authority of the United States. Lincoln was re-elected in 1864, and by the time of his second inaugural, the end of the struggle was at last in sight. In an hour of relaxation the President was stricken down by the hand of an assassin. His body was borne to his home in Springfield and to his sorrowing friends. His mortal remains now lie in a massive mausoleum which is now rapidly becoming and will long remain a World's Shrine.

AND NOW HE BELONGS TO THE AGES

FAREWELL AT SPRINGFIELD

"MY FRIENDS, NO ONE NOT IN MY SITUATION CAN APPRECIATE MY FEELING OF SADNESS AT THIS PARTING. TO THIS PLACE, AND THE KINDNESS OF THESE PEOPLE, I OWE EVERYTHING. HERE I HAVE LIVED A QUARTER OF A CENTURY, AND HAVE PASSED FROM A YOUNG TO AN OLD MAN. HERE MY CHILDREN HAVE BEEN BORN, AND ONE IS BURIED. I NOW LEAVE, NOT KNOWING WHEN OR WHETHER I EVER MAY RETURN, WITH A TASK BEFORE ME GREATER THAN THAT WHICH RESTED UPON WASHINGTON. WITHOUT THE ASSISTANCE OF THAT DIVINE BEING WHO EVER ATTENDED HIM, I CANNOT SUCCEED. WITH THAT ASSISTANCE, I CANNOT FAIL. TRUSTING IN HIM, WHO CAN GO WITH ME AND REMAIN WITH YOU, AND BE EVERYWHERE FOR GOOD, LET US CONFIDENTLY HOPE THAT ALL WILL YET BE WELL. TO HIS CARE COMMENDING YOU, AS I HOPE IN YOUR PRAYERS YOU WILL COMMEND ME, I BID YOU AN AFFECTIONATE FAREWELL."

INDEX—PERSONS AND PLACES

Advocate, Belleville 53
Advocate, Greenville .. 91, 96, 97
Aikin, George 68
Alexander, J. F. 97
Alton 153
Angle, Paul M. 119
Anna 120
Anti-Nebraska 18, 19, 20
Anti-Slavery 19
Ashley, L. W. 144

Benjamin, Judah P. 112
Bissell, Wm. H. 80, 104
Blackhawk War 9
Birkbeck, Morris 6
Boren, Hiram 108
Bowman, Kate 82
Buchanan, President 116

Cairo 114
Caledonia 108
Campaign plans 52
Campbell, Thomas 127
Cannon, the Douglas 122
Carlyle 92, 93
Cartwright, Peter 11
Carr, Clark E. 31
Carson, Will C. 96
Casey 109
Chicago Times 85
Chicago Tribune 19
Citizens, Jonesboro 117
Coles, Edward 7
Colcord, Samuel 96, 99
Colyer, Walter 63
Committee, Cairo 114
Convention, Anti-Nebraska
.... 19, 21, 111
Convention, Editorial 31
Convention, Democratic 150
Convention, Republican 154
Conger, Chauncy 62
Cooper Union Speech 154

Daimwood, Rebecca 70
Davidson, Mrs. Charles 96
Debate, three day 52
Debate, Jonesboro 127, 128
Delta and Times 82
Dickens, Charles 34
Disappointed 34
Douglas speaks 131
Dougherty, John 87

Douglas, Mrs. 143
Douglas, Stephen A.
.... 10, 14, 23-26, 94
Dubois, Jesse K. .. 49, 84, 85, 104
Dungy, William 107

"Early Engagements" 69
Egypt 33, 35
Elections-1840 51
Electors 54
Equality Debate 71

Fairfield 67
Frankland, Mrs. Anna 69
Freeport 111
French 33, 34

Gillespie, Joseph 77, 89, 120
Greenville College 92
Greeley, Horace 92

Hackers, the 87, 122
Hanna, Robert P. 66
Herald, St. Louis Daily 113
Herbert, Mrs. Oscar 109
Herndon, Wm. H. 31
Highlands 99
Hitt, Robert R. 121
House divided speech 31, 32

Indifference 120
Interrogations 138

Jefferson, Thomas 3
Joint Debate arranged 25, 27

Kenner, G. L. 110
Koerner, Gustavus 80, 90

Lackey, Joel 108
Layman, Thomas J. 107, 145
Leaders, two great 29, 30
Leecompton 22, 23, 25
Lemen, James 103
Letter 49
Lincoln 9-25,
   31, 47-66, 77-90, 135, 150-158
Linder, Usher 112
Logan, Dr. John 5
Logan, John A. 120
Logan, Stephen T. 9
Long Nine 10, 30
Looking-glass Prairie 90

157

INDEX—PERSONS AND PLACES

Maffitt, Mrs. J. W. 61
Maloney, Dr. 137
Manus, Tillman 130
Marshall, Samuel D. 68
Martin, James A. 105
Marietta, Ohio 2, 3
Mason-Dixon Line 4
McClellan, George B. 147
McClernand, John A. 57
McLean, Dr. 128
McVane, Dr. 122
Mexican War 11
"Missionaries" 55
Missouri Compromise 17, 18
Moore's Prairie 145
Morganfield, Ky. 73
Moyer, Wm. N. 108

Olney 74
Ordinance of 1787 .... 2, 3
Ottawa 111

Pace, Harvey T. 57
Park, Benjamin 75
Park Hotel 105
Personal 139
Phillips, D. L. 120
Phillips, Judson 144
Platform, Douglas' 150
Public men 39, 40

Reese, John P. 124
Republican Party 18
Robinson, John M. 61
Roughnecks 125

Salem 103
Sangamon country 5
Schuh, Mrs. Mary 109

Scott, Dred 134, 138
Senators, Southern 149
Smith, Nat 82
Smith, Wm. S. 97
Shawneetown-Public Men . 67, 70
"Sons of the South" 21
Stewart, Mary Jane 61
Squatters 21
Squatter Sovereignty 111

Tablet 58, 80, 98
Tarbell, Ida 10
Taylor House 115
Telegraph, Alton 99
Terpenitz, J. E. 114, 123
Times and Delta, Cairo 114
Tippecanoe Parade 97
Tharp, A. J. 109
Trumbull, Lyman
.... 26, 80, 83, 97, 135
Toler, Grace Cabot 109
Towns visited 46

Union Hotel 121, 123

Vermont Resolutions 138

Walker, Isaac 62
Wait, Wm. S. 91
Waterloo 113
Webb, Edwin 61
White, Horace 89, 119
Wigwam 151
Will, Conrad 5
Wilson, Prof. 144
Whigs 9, 15, 30, 31
Whitney, Henry C. 147
Wooden, W. T. 23

Shawnee Classics
A Series of Classic Regional Reprints for the Midwest

A SHAWNEE CLASSIC

It Happened in Southern Illinois
John W. Allen

Legends and Lore of Southern Illinois
John W. Allen

Kaskaskia under the French Regime
Natalia Maree Belting
New Foreword by Carl J. Ekberg

The Boy of Battle Ford and the Man
W. S. Blackman
New Introduction by Herbert K. Russell

Prairie Albion: An English Settlement in Pioneer Illinois
Charles Boewe

Personal Memoirs of John H. Brinton, Civil War Surgeon, 1861–1865
John H. Brinton
New Foreword by John Y. Simon
New Preface by John S. Haller Jr.

Behind the Guns: The History of Battery I, 2nd Regiment,
Illinois Light Artillery
Thaddeus C. S. Brown, Samuel J. Murphy, and William G. Putney
Edited with a Foreword by Clyde C. Walton

Growing Up with Southern Illinois, 1820 to 1861: From the Memoirs
of Daniel Harmon Brush
Daniel Harmon Brush
New Foreword by Michael C. Batinski

The Conquest of the Illinois
George Rogers Clark
Edited by Milo Milton Quaife
New Foreword by Rand Burnette

Stagecoach and Tavern Tales of the Old Northwest
Harry Ellsworth Cole
Edited by Louise Phelps Kellogg
New Introduction by Patrick J. Brunet

The Great Cyclone at St. Louis and East St. Louis, May 27, 1896
Compiled and Edited by Julian Curzon
New Foreword by Tim O'Neil

A Knight of Another Sort: Prohibition Days and Charlie Birger
Gary DeNeal
Foreword by Jim Ballowe

The Flag on the Hilltop
Mary Tracy Earle
Introduction by Herbert K. Russell

"Black Jack": John A. Logan and Southern Illinois in the Civil War Era
James Pickett Jones
Foreword by John Y. Simon

John A. Logan: Stalwart Republican from Illinois
James Pickett Jones

Reminiscences of a Soldier's Wife: An Autobiography
Mrs. John A. Logan
New Foreword by John Y. Simon

French and Indians of Illinois River
Nehemiah Matson
New Foreword by Rodney O. Davis

History, 31st Regiment, Illinois Volunteers Organized by John A. Logan
W. S. Morris, L. D. Hartwell, and J. B. Kuykendall
New Foreword by John Y. Simon

A History of the Ninth Regiment, Illinois Volunteer Infantry, with
the Regimental Roster
Marion Morrison
New Foreword by John Y. Simon

Tales and Songs of Southern Illinois
Collected by Charles Neely
Edited with a Foreword by John Webster Spargo

Eight Months in Illinois: With Information to Immigrants
William Oliver
New Foreword by James E. Davis

The Outlaws of Cave-in-Rock
Otto A. Rothert
New Foreword by Robert A. Clark

When Lincoln Came to Egypt
George W. Smith
New Foreword by Daniel W. Stowell

A Woman's Story of Pioneer Illinois
Christiana Holmes Tillson
Edited by Milo Milton Quaife
New Introduction by Kay J. Carr

Autobiography of Silas Thompson Trowbridge, M.D.
New Introduction by John S. Haller Jr. and Barbara Mason

Life and Letters of General W. H. L. Wallace
Isabel Wallace
New Foreword by John Y. Simon

Army Life of an Illinois Soldier: Including a Day-by-Day Record of Sherman's
March to the Sea
Charles W. Wills
Compiled by Mary E. Kellogg
New Foreword by John Y. Simon